Velcro Families: They Stick!

Velcro Families: They Stick!

LeRoy Lawson

RESOURCE *Publications* · Eugene, Oregon

VELCRO FAMILIES: THEY STICK!

Resource Publications
An Imprint of Wipf and Stock Publishers
199 W. 8th Ave., Suite 3
Eugene, OR 97401

www.wipfandstock.com

PAPERBACK ISBN: 978-1-7252-8598-9
HARDCOVER ISBN: 978-1-7252-8597-2
EBOOK ISBN: 978-1-7252-8599-6

Manufactured in the U.S.A.   06/19/23

Shawn Christopher Terrill
May 23, 1968-July 21, 1989

Lane Whitney Lawson
June 24,1967-May 26, 1994

Two admirable young sons and brothers
drawn together by the love of their fathers
nurtured by the care of their mothers
safe in the arms of their families
But in the end
overpowered by forces they could not defeat
secure forever in the love that will not let them go.

Contents

Preface

Roy and Joy Lawson Tigard, Oregon 1960

FOR SEVERAL YEARS JOY urged me to publish the story of our Velcro family. I hesitated, and for the best of reasons: I didn't know how to do it. Even now I offer these pages with some trepidation. I dared to try because Mark Taylor said he'd help. A good friend.

I still don't know how to do it for a general reading audience. It was the idea of *publishing* that stumped me for so long. This is my thirtieth book, starting with *Very Sure of God*, my revised doctoral dissertation, which came out in 1974. The last one appeared in 2004, *Conformed to His Likeness*. This one, like most of my books, was written on assignment from Standard Publishing. It was another adult Bible study for Standard's annual

Vacation Bible School program. These studies sold well, met a need, and helped me hone my research and writing skills.

In other words, I had some experience in book *writing*. What I didn't know was how to *publish* one. Or market it. These were the duties of the publisher, so I pretty much ignored them. There was something else. You can't really write a book until you define whom you are writing *for* and *to*. Aye, there's the rub: Who was my audience? Who would read a book about a Velcro family except the Velcro family? Who even knows what that is? So I procrastinated. For a long time.

Until now. I could just say that Joy wore me down. She not only has long urged me to get on with it, but she recruited other family members to add to the pressure. There were also the others. When nonfamily members heard of our experiment, several wanted to know more. "What is this thing called a Velcro family?" "How did you get started?" "How do you keep it going?" "Think I could do it?"

So over time I began secretly thinking through how to tackle the challenge. Now, at long last, I'm ready. I work best against a deadline, and a potential deadline is looming—although that may change, depending on Covid-19. I'm writing this introduction in the midst of the pandemic. We're locked in, increasingly restless with our enforced isolation. Now a date we set in 2018 seems threatened. By the time this book is completed we'll know whether we can keep it.

I'm talking about our all-family Sixtieth Anniversary Cruise. On June 11, 1960 Joy Annette Whitney changed her last name to Lawson. She and I have now weathered and mostly enjoyed six decades together. We joined forces in Oregon, left the state in 1965, and did not return to reside here permanently until February 2020. In the intervening years we formed our biological family and then, without thinking much about it in the beginning, our Velcro family.

They are the real reason I'm writing. This book is for our biological and Velcro offspring. I've tossed aside any idea of publishing a widely read book. I still think I'm right: the public at large isn't clamoring to read about our family, as wonderful as we think we are. But *we* will read it. It's *our* family story. But it's not just for our current collection. Long after Joy and I are gone—and that deadline looms pretty large when you've hit your eighties—our kids' kids and their kids will ask questions that only the contributors to this volume can answer. One of my biggest old-age regrets is that I didn't pepper my own parents with questions I didn't even know enough to ask then but am bedeviled by now.

Preface

That deadline I mentioned several meandering sentences ago is rapidly approaching. Thanksgiving week, 2020. That's it. Most of our whole big Velcro family will be cruising together on the Caribbean (over 60 of us at last count). We did this once before, for my seventieth birthday. That time forty-three of us sailed for a week along the Mexican Riviera. That was when we discovered that cruising may be the most economical, most convenient, and most rewarding way to bring a few dozen people from several states and two countries together, keep them fed and entertained for a week, and help them build memories and cement relationships for a lifetime.

We had such a good time in 2008 we're going to do it again—the pandemic permitting. Joy and I couldn't think of a better way to party for our anniversary than to gather up our brood once again and go sailing, this time south from New Orleans. That cruise is my deadline. I want the book ready to distribute by then.

What you just read was the truth when I wrote it, especially the part that says, "the pandemic permitting." Well, the pandemic didn't permit. In July 2020 I sent an email to the family postponing the cruise. Covid-19 was once again on a rampage, with no signs of abating in time for us to sail in November. So—the cruise is off, but the publication deadline hasn't changed. I still hope to deliver copies of this book to the family in November. Then maybe—the pandemic permitting—we can cruise together next year. In the meantime, enjoy reading.

Introduction and Timeline

WHERE TO BEGIN? YOU can skip this introduction if you'd like. It wasn't in the manuscript I sent off to my good friend Mark Taylor, who agreed to edit the book. I used to work for Mark when he was editor of *Christian Standard*, for which I wrote a monthly column, "From My Bookshelf" for nine years. He was a gentle editor, treating my offerings with tender loving care—while at the same time making certain they were up to *Standard's* standard.

I knew I could trust him to be honest with me. And boy, honest he was! His manner was predictably kind, but he tactfully, cautiously, but also rather pointedly suggested a number of changes to improve my initial offering. One specific improvement: maybe if I would attach an introduction, you, dear reader, might be able to make some sense of the book itself. Try as he might, he said, he couldn't keep from getting lost in the names—"so *many* names."

And—he didn't actually say this but hinted—"so many *years*." I've lived so long he got confused trying to figure out what happened when and where. You need to give us a *timeline*, he said. Well, not quite so bluntly. Here's how he put it: "Perhaps it would be good to include with this intro a simple timeline of your life: early days, education, ministries, retirement activities."

I hesitated, because the book is about the Velcro Family, not the *pater familias*. (Although I like the label. *Wikipedia* explains it: "The *pater familias*, also written as *paterfamilias*, was the head of a Roman family. The *pater familias* was the oldest living male in a household, and exercised autocratic authority over his extended family." It's that "autocratic authority" part that I like. You'll discover if you read any further, though, that I could never pull it off. I can huff and puff all I want. My family will listen respectfully, pat me on the head, and go ahead and do whatever they had in mind to do.)

1

Anyway, please forgive me for what follows here. I'm only doing it because Mark said to. It's arranged by both chronology and geography, so you'll know when and where the events took place. Then when you are wandering through the thicket of names and stories that follow, you can turn back to this timetable to discover where you are.

Oregon 1938–1965

1938–1956. Tillamook. Born and raised in this small coastal town. Son of Elmer LaVerne Lawson and Margery Evelyn Foltz Eastwood Lawson. Brother of older sister Betty Jeanne and younger brother John David. My father's firstborn, my mother's second. This makes me both a firstborn and a squeeze child. Explains a lot.

Velcro

- Aunt Betty and her children. (Not really Velcro, since we're "blood kin," but later I explain why we think they also belong as "Velcro")
- Widmer families
- Jacob Families
- Faye and Lorraine Filby

Later adoptees in Oregon:

- Loretta Green
- Brenda and Tony Painchaud

1956–1960. Eugene. Northwest Christian College. B.A. (Bachelor of Arts in Theology)

1957–59. Portland. Weekend youth minister at St. Johns Christian Church. Some of the kids in my youth group were older than I. But I could talk faster.

1959–1965 Tigard. Pastor, Villa Ridge and Tigard Christian Church (Same church, relocated to a new place and name in 1964). I still admire the brave souls and genuine saints who came Sunday after Sunday to listen to their young pastor practice preaching at their expense. I never served the church full time. By the time it was large enough to support a pastor, I felt God's call to "go from your country, your people and your father's household to the land I will show you." For Abraham that meant the Promised Land. For the Lawsons it meant Tennessee, which was pretty promising also.

1960. Portland. Banner year. Graduated from Northwest Christian College with a B.A. in theology. But the really big event: Married Joy Annette Whitney. From this point on the story is about *us*, since whatever I have done has been with her encouragement and partnership. "As it was in the beginning, 'tis now and ever shall be' until . . ."

1960–962. Portland. Cascade College A.B. (Bachelor of Arts in English, 1962). The original plan had been to go "back East" for a graduate seminary degree after two years as Villa Ridge's pastor, when the congregation would call a real minister to lead. But I fell in love with the people and couldn't leave. Instead, I picked up a second undergraduate degree along with teaching credentials, in case I couldn't make it as a preacher.

Velcros

- Terrills. Today there are three generations of them (Jeff and Joan; Kim, Kristin, and Shawn [deceased]; Madi, Cade, Joel, Derek). As you'll discover, others enter the story before Jeff and Joan, but it was the bond between Jeff and his pastor that is the identifiable beginning of the Velcro family experience.

1962–65. Portland. Reed College. M.A.T. (Master of Arts in Teaching, 1965). Since I couldn't bring myself to leave the church, I went to work on my master's degree, still planning on a future seminary degree. According to Reed, my two undergraduate schools weren't up to standard, so I was admitted on probation. If I could pass two of their classes, they'd let me in. I passed. Some members of the church were afraid I might lose my faith in that "secular, radical" college. I didn't.

1962–64. Tigard. English teacher, Tigard Union High School. I'd have taught here longer, but the church grew and I became overextended: full-time teacher, part-time preacher, graduate school student, husband, and new father. My performance was less than brilliant in all of these jobs.

Pre-Velcro:

- Carole Boyd

1963. Portland. Kimberly Joy was born. (Remember her middle name.) I fell in love with her when she was brand new and never got over it.

1964–1968. Portland/Indianapolis. Candidate secretary, Christian Missionary Fellowship. Another part-time job. It entailed helping recruit and prepare missionaries for field service. When I left Tigard Union High School, I was an active substitute teacher in the system for a year, but I needed a little more income to support our growing family. CMF's office was in Indianapolis, but mine was in our home. My assigned territory was the United States. At my 1964 birthday Joy presented me with a suitcase. *Hmmm*, thought I. *What's she trying to tell me?*

1965. Portland. Candace Annette was born. (Notice her middle name.) I was apprehensive before she arrived. Could I ever love another child as much as I loved Kim? I could. I did. I do. Candy was born thirteen days before her move to Tennessee. (I know, I know. All the mothers we have known since have charged, "How could you?!")

Tennessee 1965–1973

1965–1973. Johnson City. Milligan College: assistant professor of English, chair of the English department, chair of the Humanities Program, and vice president.

1967. Johnson City. Lane Whitney Lawson was born. (Notice the middle name. Joy's full name, you'll recall, was Joy Annette Whitney. Her mother's maiden name was Lane. At this point in our marriage Joy had used up all her names. It was my turn. That's when Joy told me there would be no more children. And I had so many good ones: my father, Elmer LaVerne; his father, Pearl Redfern; and his father, Alonzo. What a loss! All these perfectly good family names would now never be handed down.) Once again I learned that love is big enough to take in another child, and what a child!

1968–70 Nashville. Vanderbilt University. Ph.D. English. This move was a bit of a challenge, since I went off salary from Milligan College but still had five mouths to feed. Thanks to a teaching fellowship from Vanderbilt and several part-time jobs, we made it. Those jobs: choir director, Eastwood Christian Church; manager, Morgan House apartments for married students; garbage man (I hired myself. I also hired Joy to prepare apartments for new residents. She scrubbed eighty-five ovens that year. And never complained.)

Pre-Velcro

- Sharman Bean

1970–73. Johnson City. Vice president, Milligan College. I returned to a new job at Milligan, administrative assistant to the president, the Number Two position in the administration. My title was later changed to vice president. When the local newspaper announced the change, a bank teller friend asked about it. I explained it was the same position, just a new title. She understood. "Oh, we do that all the time in the bank. Give a new title instead of a raise."

Indiana 1973–1979

1973–1979. Indianapolis. Senior minister, East Thirty-Eighth Street Christian Church (now Post Road Christian Church). I was pretty nervous about this call. In Tennessee I'd served as interim minister at East Unaka Christian Church in Johnson City and Colonial Heights Christian Church in Kingsport as well as guest preaching elsewhere pretty regularly, but East Thirty-Eighth was a large church with an attendance of 800–900 each Sunday; Tigard Christian's was only about 120 when we left Oregon. I had a lot to learn. Since then I've often referred to the Indianapolis ministry as my lab course. They were patient with me as I bumbled around. For the first year I just tried to figure out how my predecessor, E. Ray Jones, did things and then copied him!

Velcro

- Carolyn Webster

Arizona and California 1979–2003

1979–1999. Mesa. Senior minister, Central Christian Church. We were surprised when the cochairman of Central's search committee called to ask me to consider becoming their pastor. The Lawsons—in the desert? We're from Oregon, remember. "I'm not asking you to give me an answer now," he said. "I just want you to pray about it." What am I going to say, "No, I won't pray about it"? So Joy and I prayed. The rest is history.

Velcro

- Brian Matlock
- Mike Prior
- Rosa Viteri
- Patti and Richard Phillips
- Darrin and Julie Ronde
- Barbara and Karinna Domke
- Casey and Jayne Reynolds. And their children (and in some cases, grandchildren).

Almost Velcro

- Steven Ostrega

1990–2003 Fullerton. President, Hope International University (formerly Pacific Christian College). Yes, you read the dates right. We were in our eleventh year in Mesa when the trustees of Pacific Christian College in Fullerton, California, asked me to become president. "I can't," I told them. "I have this church so far in debt if I were to leave now you couldn't respect me and I couldn't respect myself." So they went away. But in time they came back, "OK, don't leave, but come anyway." That was tantalizing enough to hook me. For nine more years I continued pastoring in Mesa while presidenting in Fullerton. Then, after retiring from the church, I stayed on with the college (by then Hope International University) for four more years.

Memorial Day Weekend 1994

This date changed our lives forever. Our son, Lane, just weeks short of 27, took his own life. For years he had been battling his health. Doctors pinned various labels on his condition, but the most accurate seemed to be neurochemical depression brought on by his allergy to petrochemicals. The chemicals were everywhere: the automotive-exhaust-polluted air he breathed, most of the clothes he wore, the fabrics he sat on, and so much more. He moved from the Phoenix area to the coast of southern Oregon in search of purer air. For a while he felt better. Then he didn't.

Rootless 2003–4

My work with Hope International University concluded in May 2003. We sold our house and bought a motor home, sold the car, and bought a pickup truck to tow behind the motorhome—I needed something for hauling the Harley (retirement gift from Central Christian), and for about a year-and-a-half we toured America. That's a book in itself. It was won-derful, mostly, except that the aging motor home never gave us more than two consecutive days without something breaking. In my guest speaking toward the end of our tour I included something like this: "I've been com-missioned to make a study of RV repair shops in America and I'm just about ready to submit my report." In spite of the frustrations—and there were many for this dedicated nonmechanic—I'd like to do it again. Joy expresses a slightly different opinion.

2004–2011 Arizona Again

Payson. While motor homing we sized up everywhere we visited as a possi-ble future normal retirement home. We hadn't found any place satisfactory until we returned to Arizona in the summer of 2004. I parked Joy and the motor home in the mountain town of Payson, where we had lived during some of our Mesa years (when Joy was also in search of cleaner air) and at-tended the North American Christian Convention in Phoenix. I was still in the Valley when she phoned to announce she'd found a condo. Would I look at it? I came, I saw, and the condo conquered. It became our home until 2011. As we moved in, I went to work once again for Christian Missionary Fellowship, this time as international consultant. My new boss, Doug Priest, asked me to list the things I was doing (guest speaking, column writing, article publishing, church consulting). Then he said simply, "Now do these things for CMF." That was my new part-time position's job description, one I enjoyed until I retired again in 2019. In 2007 I also served several months as interim pastor of Scottsdale Christian Church in the Valley.

Tennessee Again 2012–2016

Johnson City. Distinguished professor, Emmanuel Christian Seminary. (The "distinguished" is an honorific bestowed, I'm pretty sure, because of my age—not because of my demeanor.) During fall semester 2010 I substituted a semester for a Milligan College professor on sabbatical. Dr. Mike Sweeney, president of Emmanuel, offered me a job pending faculty approval, of course. It came, and I accepted. Emmanuel's was one of my best assignments. I didn't really want to retire again from this slot when I did, even though I was less than impressed with my performance. (I was no longer young, you see, and there's this memory issue.) During my last year with Emmanuel I also did a five-month stint as the interim pastor of First Christian Church in Johnson City, another real blessing.

Would Be Velcro—except for Their Functional Families

- Adam Tomlinson
- Kaitlyn Harville

Homeless Again 2016–2020

Lawsonsontheloose.net. When we left Emmanuel and First Christian, we once again divested ourselves and took off for parts unknown. When we had retired in California, we put our pared-down furnishings in storage. This time we gave everything away to our kids and grandkids and friends—cars, furniture, other household goods, clothes, personal items—almost everything. I kept only a couple cabinets of work papers and Joy only her art supplies. We stored them in the Jacob's barn in Oregon. And we took off. We traveled with only what we could contain in a suitcase, a carry-on, and a personal item apiece. We didn't own a key to anything. For nearly four years we were all over the globe, eventually boasting that in our lifetime together we'd been to all seven continents and fifty states. In 2019 we began making plans to settle. In 2020 we barely made it back to the States before the Covid-19 pandemic hit. We were glad to be home.

Oregon, Finally

February 2020 to the present. Senior associate pastor, Northwest Christian Church, Newberg, Oregon. During the interview for this position, I asked what my title would be. The response: "We're considering either Gandalf or Yoda."

Joy's choice: "Yoda. You look like Yoda."

There's some irony here. From the joke you can tell they were hiring me for my so-called "wisdom and experience." But I have very little to offer. Like every baby born with no experience in the place he's entering, Joy and I have moved into a world we've never been in before. For one thing, what I thought I knew about ministry is pretty dated. The whole world has gone digital now. And so much of the population feels so different about the church and even God. I've had to learn new ways of communicating and relating.

And then came the Covid-19 pandemic. I haven't been through a lockdown before, haven't had to do church online before, haven't tried to take care of hurting or dying people I couldn't get to in person. I wasn't even supposed to hold their hands while praying for them. I'm persuaded that on the other side of this pandemic we won't return to business as we used to do it, even church business. So much for my wisdom and experience!

In this uneven exchange, though, I came out on top. I get to learn new skills, gain new experience, work with an excellent team—and get paid for it.

David Case is the senior pastor of NCC. He's the real reason the call to Newberg tempted me. I've known him for decades. I knew he was smart when he married Julie Hoven. Let me tell you his wonderful story.

David didn't come from a Christian family and hadn't ever gone to church when he began trying to date Julie. Her parents said she couldn't go out with him unless he would come to church with her. Well, she was cute, and he was enamored, and going to church was a small price to pay. Besides, he also loved to play basketball—and the church had a gym.! So he began attending, and he captured Julie, and the Lord captured him. He became a leader in the youth group, then the youth minister, and in time the senior minister of the only church he has ever attended. I don't know of another story like his.

And that elder? He's ElDon Hoven, my second oldest friend in the world. We became next-door neighbors when he was seven and I was five. Who would have guessed we'd be together again over seventy years later? What a treat.[1]

---

1. This brings to an end the timeline you asked for, Mark Taylor. I hope it is what you had in mind.

Part 1

Meet Our Velcro Family

1

But First, a Word from Our DNA Family

I'M DOING MOST OF the talking in this book. That's only fair, since Joy insisted I write it and since I enter the story before anyone else. But it would be incomplete without her say. You'll notice she is not as wordy as I am.

Joy's Perspective

Who are these folks who collect Velcro kids?

It is said, "Opposites attract." That's true of Roy and me. I grew up with a twin brother and warm, nurturing parents. One of my favorite memories is a call from Daddy to gather for a Milford Monkey story. In front of the fireplace with me on one side of his lap and my brother, Dan, on the other side, he held us captive by recounting the adventures of a very curious little monkey. Even as teenagers we clamored for more. It was so much fun.

My brother was my best friend, very protective of me, even helping me choose boyfriends. Our parents were trusting of both of us. I think of one story in particular to illustrate how we worked to keep their trust. The day after our high school graduation Dan and I were invited to a graduation party at the lake. We soon learned that the purpose of the party was to get the preacher's kids drunk, and our friends told us they would tell our parents they saw us drunk. What would our parents think of us then? We did not succumb to the pressure and assured them we were telling the folks about the goals of the party. Driving home they were scared they would get into trouble and we were scared we would get stopped by a cop and be arrested with the rest of them.

My folks were a little unsure of themselves away from home, so we kept close to each other and shared a lot of love within the family.

Roy was both a first child and a second child in his family. His mother had a five-year-old girl when she married Roy's father. He was his father's first child. Four years later his brother was born, which made Roy the middle child. His family was falling apart during his teen years, so he had to look outside his core family for the support he needed.

The Tillamook Christian Church took this smart, nerdy, gregarious, needy kid and got him involved in everything that would nurture his talents and encourage his spirit. This taught him to see the world as a great support system outside the family. His parents divorced during his senior year, so the church gave him a scholarship to college. His social popularity continued through college. He was president of the student body when we met.

I first laid eyes on Roy when I was in junior high. I attended a state church youth convention at the time he was just entering the Oregon Christian Endeavor leadership team. His first position was sergeant at arms. I witnessed the sergeant at arms become the hit of the convention as he turned the "Lost and Found" announcements into a comedy routine.

Four years later our family met Roy on the sidewalk as we were moving my twin brother into his college dorm. Miss Wallflower greets Mr. Popular. He says it was "love at first sight." I said, "Nice and friendly guy." I saw no future.

Our first date was the freshman reception. It was the student body president's job to introduce each freshman to the college president, Dr. Griffith, who stood first in the faculty line. Roy took me through the line first and then it was Miss Wallflower's privilege to admire him as he gregariously made introductions. His second role was to be master of ceremonies for the program. I was in awe of it all.

The attraction for me was Roy's strong connection to all those around him. Roy's attraction to me was my strong family relationships. I took him home for Thanksgiving because he had no family to go home to. That sealed the deal for him. He wanted in on this family stuff. He asked my father for my hand. I can see my Daddy grinning even now. At the college's Christmas formal we announced our engagement. In June we were married.

Our first home was the attic of the little church Roy had started the previous July. That room was sixteen by ten feet—and we could stand up only in the middle of the sloped ceiling. The downstairs church kitchen and bathrooms were ours during the week, and the parishioners invited us to lunch on Sunday.

Our first Velcro relationship began about two years later as we began building a relationship with Jeff and his mother, Lillian. We invited them to dinner, they invited us to dinner, he went water skiing with Jeff, and I got cooking lessons and a love for antiques from Jeff's mom. They came to church, and our church family also took them in: inviting them to picnics, reroofing their house, welcoming them to Bible study, enjoying their curiosity, and just accepting them as they were.

The Velcro concept began to take form here. From then on, wherever we lived, kids who needed a family found us.

It wasn't until our son Lane died that our far-flung family of kids met each other. The loss of Lane was a loss to all of us. The bonding began, and the annual family vacation was born. The first summer, 1995, Jeff brought all the water toys for daytime fun at the lake, and our evening bonfires with singing, joking, stories, tears, and hugs glued us together. Family traditions were begun, and each year since then the family has grown because we want others to find acceptance in the crazy, loving family that has helped put all of us back together when we needed it most.

What does the Velcro family mean to me?

We are a minister's family, but God has not exempted us from the skirmishes of life on this earth. We need the Velcro family as much as they need us. Roy has sons to play with, bond with, learn from, and work with since our Lane no longer can. I love the gathering of family on any occasion. To see our home full of joy, love, and acceptance even when we are struggling with the deepest of losses helps bring us back to life. To see light come back into the eyes of any of our family members brings brighter eyes to all of us.

One of the greatest joys of the Velcro family has been watching our DNA kids take them all in, too. At our gatherings it would be hard to tell which ones were physically born to us. They are in the middle of it all, supporting anyone who needs support or just having fun with them. I've never seen a sign of any jealously. I think they are grateful to have help with their quirky old folks.

Kim: The Big Sister's Take

The Thompson family 1984: (left to right) Ed, Kim, Luke (now 27), Bre (now 31), Nicholas (now 29), Kyle (now 31), and Nick (now 29)

Doesn't everybody have a Velcro family? Isn't it natural to invite people into your lives as family? It always seemed so to me. I didn't know any different!

As a child we always seemed to have people coming and going all the time. I remember Sharman living with us in Tennessee, Hap living with us in Indiana, Carolyn in Indiana. Then I started the inviting. But it wasn't just people living with us. We often had dinner guests. Sunday dinner often included someone Mom and Dad invited to join us after church. As missionaries came to town, often we would host them for dinner or even let them stay overnight with us for a few days. Dad also seemed to know people from everywhere through his travels and ministry work, which led to company often.

Mom was the gracious hostess who made an environment that was always warm and welcoming. It never crossed my mind that someone I invited would not be welcome. So, of course, when my friend's dad died and her mom had to take a job in another city in the middle of the school semester, she should stay with us. It never occurred to me that there could be another option. If we could make it work, we should make it work. This

16

is the story of my life. Fortunately, my parents agreed. They had set a precedent. They didn't have to choose everyone to invite. I could do it too! And I did! Over and over again.

I love my parents. Not many parents are willing to accept all the kids you drag home as their own. Not just playmates or social acquaintances but as real family. The people you do life with. The people who really know you and love you anyway.

I can't imagine a different family!

Candace: How the Younger Sister Sees It

Candace and Michael Ohanessian, Melbourne, Australia

It's important that proper acknowledgement finally be given me regarding the Velcro situation. The sacrifices I've personally made have been tremendous, allowing these strangers to enter my family, showing up year after year without so much as a "by your leave." My forbearance is, hmmm, dare I say heroic? All that unconditional love I've had to endure, that humor that lightened my suffering, and vital support when I most needed it. That kind of stuff really wears on a person.

I remember coming to family vacation year after year when I was deep in my addiction. I was emotionally guarded and shockingly thin, and sometimes prone to lash out when I felt judged or threatened (and I felt judged and threatened a lot). But although I was spoiling for a fight, it's hard to fight when all you get is love in return. It was difficult for me to come some years, but at the same time I couldn't stay away. Something in me feared the unconditional love yet craved it at the same time.

When I finally cleaned myself up, ah, the warmth and joy I felt from you all. Jeff, thank you for coming to see me in rehab, an old drunk and young (well, young-*ish*) tweaker, what a pair we made. You understood me as only someone who's been in my shoes can. You showed me there is no shame in one's past and that in fact it can become a gift. I don't think you know what a blessing you were for me then, and you are for me still today.

And my divorce! I don't think any of us understand what David did (I mean c'mon, leaving *me??*), but you once again held me close, and embraced the next fella I dragged home. Michael was instantly part of the family, and he has grown to love you as much as I do.

This thing we've got going is really something, considering what an odd bunch of humans we are. I am confounded by many of the things you think and say and believe and do, maybe as much as you are confounded by the things I think and say and believe and do, but we just keep coming together and hugging and loving. At the end of the day, we know each others' hearts, and all is well.

So there it is. You loved me unconditionally when my life was a mess, held me tight through my recovery and shock divorce, and celebrated with me as I put my life back together, finding my feet and finding love again. You held me through it all, so that I can hold others as they go through their own difficulties. You've given me warmth, stories, fellowship and laughter, always the laughter. Every single one of you has made my life richer for having you in it. You've got a lot to answer for.[1]

---

1. Or, as Eminent Grammarian Reverend Professor Doctor Lawson Sir would say, "There is a plenitude of items for which a response from you is obligatory." This footnote has been provided by Candace herself.

Lane, the Youngest

Lane Lawson's last Christmas, 1993

Lane is not here to tell his own story, but I'd like you to know about him—in his mother's words.

"We gotta boy!"

Our one fear was two older sisters might make a sissy out of Lane. At two years old he erased our fears when, peering out of the car window, he began imitating the growling roar of the trucks passing by. Boys must have car noise instincts. He sure didn't learn that from his sisters. When it came time to play house we wondered what his response would be. Not wanting to be left out, he ran to the other room, grabbed a book, and returned to announce, "I have the book, so I'm Daddy."

As our youngest, he was privileged to be the only child for a few hours a day until he went to preschool at four. He was a great companion, so I took him everywhere. When we went to the paint store they called him "Smiley." He always brought a smile to us then. Even now I linger on the happy memories. When he was about four we had a family outing to get milkshakes. Lane was so excited that he soon spilled his. He looked down and said, "I'm just a problem drinker."

Lane's medical problems began at about eight years old. Our "Smiley" at times would say, "Nobody likes me" and go hide in his bedroom tent.

Later when playing junior high football, tackling was his favorite part of the sport. But if he cheated on his special diet (Feingold Diet for hyperactive kids) he didn't know which end of the field was his team's, and if anyone hit him he was in tears. Our even-tempered Lane had to work harder than we knew to keep his mind and moods where he wanted them to be.

As a teenager he found the kids on the periphery and included them in his life. His best buds gave these kids the same respect Lane did. We still see some of them from time to time and our encounter is always very warm. The mention of Lane brings warm fuzzies to all of us.

Lane was a good student, and his German teacher made him apply for a yearlong scholarship to be part of the German government exchange program. He received the award. He loved the year, but then he had to return home to his world of mostly teenagers. He wanted to share his new worldview, but there were no peers who could relate to that bigger world. They still wanted to be teenagers.

After a stint in Northern Arizona University in Flagstaff, he applied to work for AT&T. While waiting in the store to be interviewed, he sold a typewriter and a phone. He got the job! He loved selling, but the workplace air was so toxic to him he went home sick every night. After two years he was put on disability, and he came back to Arizona from where he was working in Buffalo, New York.

Because the Arizona air pollution was also so troubling to his health, he asked to go to Oregon and live on Grandpa Whitney's beach property. He had always loved Oregon. He began to take tai chi classes, hoping to strengthen his mind. He won several medals at state and district martial arts competitions. But after he contracted Lyme disease, his mind and body failed him.

He was always the first one to come home for Christmas, decorate the tree, and even help with making Christmas goodies. He loved being home for the holidays but did have to get back to Oregon for the January 1 Polar Bear Swim. Challenging himself seemed to be part of his healing strategy. He was even taking piano lessons.

He would have loved our family vacations, and they would have been even richer his with presence. But his absence has inspired us to love each other as we loved him.

2

The Prequel

LONG AGO, BEFORE THE Velcro family existed, before Joy and I had met, and certainly before we had adopted the term—so long ago that you couldn't even buy the real Velcro because it wasn't on the market yet—I belonged to such a family. I was a teenager. My parents' marriage had been unraveling for years leading up to their final split during my senior year of high school. Vivian Mondhan was our church's secretary and education minister. She hadn't been on the church staff many years when the husband of Grace McNeil, longtime church organist, suddenly died. Viv made a pastoral call on Grace. She continued to encourage her through the mourning period. In time, Grace invited Viv to move into the McNeil home for company (and to help the underpaid Viv with living expenses.) They remained together until Grace died many years later.

Viv and Grace took many of us teenagers under their wing. Aware of the tensions at the Lawson house, they gave me special attention. When I declared my intention to go into the ministry, Viv became my mentor, helping our minister Aldis Webb shape me up for college and a future life as a pastor. Aldis provided the inspiration and example; Viv explained the "nuts and bolts," helped me write my first sermon, guided me in my local and area Christian Endeavor leadership roles, and did her best to sand off my rough edges. (The job proved too big for her; those edges are with me to this day.) In later years Viv said she had to have her office work finished by 3:30, because that's when we teenagers (this one in particular) would drop by the church after school. Then we became her priority.

Viv's impact on my life was indelible. She was also a favorite with the Lawson kids, as was Grace. They looked to them as "Aunt Viv and Grace," although they always referred to them as VivandGrace. One name served for both. That's pretty accurate, since before my kids were born Viv became a surrogate mother to me and Grace was like her older sister. As a teenager I didn't move in with them, though I remember staying over a few nights when things were pretty tense at home. They made certain I always had a port in a storm. On trips back to Tillamook from college—and from wherever we lived after Joy and I were married—we always looked up VivandGrace.

So they taught me without knowing it what it means to be a Velcro family. And Tillamook First Christian Church illustrated the African proverb, "It takes a village to raise a child." The church was my village; VivandGrace were the special adults in my village who made sure this child would be OK.

That's the spirit of our Lawson Velcro family. We want to make sure everybody's OK.

While we're in Tillamook, let me shine the spotlight on Joy's and my roots in this town. I was born here; Joy was born in Portland and never lived here. But in recent years she has often referred to Tillamook as her hometown also. Over our sixty years together she's been back so often with me that she belongs there as much as I do. The towns of her childhood and youth (Portland, Eugene, Port Orford) did not make the lasting impression on her that her adopted Tillamook has. The following chapter introduces some of the reasons both of us love this small town. Each one is another special person.

3

George and JoAnn Widmer

George and JoAnn

THE WIDMERS HAVE BEEN my friends almost my whole life. Even before
George and JoAnn and I were friends, I was an admirer of JoAnn's parents. They were prominent leaders in my home church and town. I think
her father, A. J., was mayor when I was quite young. I know for certain he
was on the school board and chaired it awhile. He owned the Tillamook
Ford Motor Company, where my dad bought all his cars. A. J. caught my

attention when I was a boy because one of his legs was at least four inches shorter than the other. I'd never seen that before. He walked with a crutch and a platform for the foot of his short leg to rest on, but it didn't slow him down a bit. He also had a strong bass voice, and a favorite memory from those days was listening to him and his daughter Shirley sing duets in church. The one I remember most clearly was "In the Garden," when their bass and contralto voices merged with such power. It takes a lot to hold a wiggly boy's attention; these two could do it.

I didn't know either JoAnn or George well in our childhood; they were much older than I—seven years. George and my sister Betty were friends. The three of them remained close until Betty died. JoAnn was quiet, but we all learned not to let her quietness mislead. She was one strong lady. George fell for her when they were teenagers; she was the only girlfriend he ever had.

George and JoAnn became our close friends years after Joy and I left Oregon. We returned to Tillamook from time to time to visit my mother and stepfather, who had married when I was in college and never left town. It took me awhile to accept this arrangement. Jack Alcott, a meat cutter, had worked in my father's grocery store. The year Dad lost his business and moved to Portland he also lost his marriage. Mom would not move with him. Instead, she took a job as housekeeper. I wasn't around when she and Jack started dating; I also wasn't around when they married. Mom told me later she was uncertain whether I would attend, so she didn't invite me.

Anyway, about twenty-five years later it was apparent that Jack—who by this time had become a favorite of ours, and who was considerably older than my mother—was dying, so Joy and I flew from Arizona to Tillamook to be with her during Jack's final days. George and JoAnn invited us and my older sister, Betty, to stay in their home. They got more of us than they bargained for, since Jack lingered on life support for a couple of weeks.

During those days we recognized that that Mom's dementia had progressed so far that she would be unable to live alone. So while Jack's life slowly ebbed away in the hospital, we made arrangements for Mom to be moved into the Tillamook Care Center (where for years she was to receive excellent care). Then their mobile home had to be emptied (it was unlivable), their dog put to sleep (he had terrible skin cancer—he was the primary reason the mobile home had become unlivable), and the shell of the mobile home disposed of. George provided a huge burning hole for the unusable items we had to burn.

There were many other details to be taken care of. So on and on we stayed with George and JoAnn. For years afterward George reminded me that he had kept a tally of how many days I owed him and that he and JoAnn fully intended to get even. They never did.

That stay cemented our relationship. From then on they were simply a part of the family. We couldn't really make it official, since both of them came from such solid homes and they themselves raised their five children in what couldn't have been a more wholesome, nurturing family environment. But—we took them in anyway, not because of their need but because of ours. And now after twenty-five years as Velcro family, we couldn't imagine giving up George.

We did have to give up JoAnn. In 2016, when Joy and I were in Australia on the first leg of our four years as Lawsonsontheloose,[1] we got a call from Tillamook. JoAnn was dying. Fourth-stage pancreatic cancer. They thought she had only days to live. Would I come home and do her funeral? There could be only one answer. So we boarded a plane and headed north. Once again we had to extend our stay (although this time it would be with Brad and Gretchen Jacob). When her doctor explained his diagnosis, JoAnn asked, "How much time do I have?" He answered, "From three weeks to three months."

"I'll take three weeks," she told him. She lived only a short time longer. A woman of deep faith, she was not in the least afraid of death. What she didn't want was to just hang on and put her family through the trauma of a delayed departure. So she quit eating and prepared to go. After a while, though, her hospice visitor (she remained at home, slept in her own bed, attended by her faithful husband and children) told her that not eating wouldn't hasten her death, so she might as well eat. "Okay," she said, "I'll have peppermint ice cream." And that constituted her diet from then on.

Between Jack Alcott's passing and our moving my mother into her care center and JoAnn's passing in 2016, the Widmers gave the Lawsons some of our fondest memories. And from our first Velcro family vacation in Cultus Lake, Oregon in 1995 until JoAnn died, she and George were with

1. Lawsonsontheloose.net was the blog we published every week or two during our nearly four years as vagabonds all over the globe. When we weren't on the road, we stayed with Kim and Ed Thompson in the States and with Candy and Michael Ohanessian, our biological daughter and son-in-law, in both Melbourne, Australia and London, England, commuting back and forth every six weeks. They had a guest room in both locations. If you're going to travel as we did, it helps to have strategically situated relatives with a guest room!

us for almost every one. George still is, when we meet in Tillamook. As a matter of fact, George has already put his deposit down for our Sixtieth Anniversary Cruise. He'll be with us, accompanied by son Mark and daughter-in-law Pam Widmer. They are coming along to make certain George will be okay. He will be, even though he'll be 89. He is perpetually OK, or as he always insists, "Fantastic!"

In another way George is always with us. Our Velcro family vacation evenings close around a bonfire, where we tell stories and insult one another. Each year the festivities began to taper off when George announced, "JoAnn's tired. We're going home." JoAnn was never tired. George was. Now, when some of us family members are together somewhere, when it is time to leave one of us will announce, "JoAnn's tired. We're going home."

Kim insists I tell you one more Widmer memory: the "Gooey Duck" song. George is a most enthusiastic if not always melodious singer. With uncertain pitch but ample volume he would annually regale us with his rendition of the song, appropriately illustrated by the huge gooey duck clam he hauled out of his freezer to our horrified delight. (A gooey duck looks like a bloated tongue that escaped its much too small shell and could never, even if thawed out, be stuffed back in. The children were enthralled. Their parents less so.)

George Talks Back

The first time I met Roy was probably in the late 1930s, and I did not see him because I was not looking down. I was looking straight ahead, and he was probably only about two feet tall. Our love for each other has expanded over the years, especially with the Velcro family. I have no idea how I got into the Velcro family. It just happened. When this all started, I was probably one of the very first ones. But it has been a wonderful experience to be included in such a wonderful experience. It has been a great trip all through the years, and I am so happy Roy has included me in his family. I have probably known him longer than anyone, but that is a plus.

JoAnn also knew Roy for eighty some years. I lived just down the road from Roy when I was in grade school and he was in the store with his dad. I used to go with my dad to take the milk to the factory. The factory was right across the street from Roy's grocery store. Roy was in the store being a cashier. At first I did not see him, but he stood on a bushel box and checked out people's groceries. Amazing.

One thing I really remember the most is going on a whitewater float down the Deschutes River on family vacation. We were in about four rafts and we got into a big water fight. I jumped in another raft and I tried to throw Jeff into the river, but instead I got thrown into the river.

For several years, JoAnn and I went to Mesa to Roy's church. The church in Mesa was always fun to go to. We especially enjoyed attending the annual senior adult convention there. JoAnn and I would take the trailer down from Tillamook and stay on the back lot at the church and go to most of the sessions. It was fun.

I remember one time Roy could not get his motorcycle started. We worked and worked and worked on it to try to get it to start. We finally found out he had not turned on the gas.[2]

We also went to Fullerton to work at Pacific Christian College. We went with Moe and Barb Burris, and in the evenings, we would meet with Roy and Joy and several other people and go for hikes. For several years, Jeff Terrill was the head of maintenance.

Roy, do you remember the time we watched the Super Bowl in your bedroom, about eight or ten of us laying on your bed to watch the game, because your only TV was in your bedroom?[3]

Roy took about forty of us on a cruise from Los Angeles to Mexico for his seventieth birthday. The sixtieth wedding anniversary cruise will be our third cruise with Roy and Joy.

I remember when Roy was a junior or senior in high school. He went to Washington, D.C. to speak to the United Nations (Roy can correct if that

2. It was worse than George says. He and his best friend, Ted Jacob, came to our house, a couple of blocks from the church, so I could show off my new-used Honda Shadow. Beautiful bike. It had a short somewhere that drained the battery, so on this day when it wouldn't start, I thought that was the problem. Ordinarily a quick push did the trick. George and Ted agreed to push me. They pushed to the end of the block and back again. Still it wouldn't kick in. They were panting and sweating and red in the face. These were old men, around 70 at the time. As they caught their breath, I saw that I had inadvertently turned the lever on the gas line to the off position. No wonder it couldn't start. No fuel!

3. It's amazing what some people remember! I was away. Joy went ahead and invited the family members in town over to the house to watch the Super Bowl game. We had another TV, but the best one was in our bedroom, so that's where the party took place. It was all in the family, after all.

is incorrect)[4], and he was also president of the Christian Endeavor for the Oregon Coast.[5]

Roy, you have my permission to correct anything that is not right.[6]

George and JoAnn have a large family, each of their five children and their children deserving a section. In recent years, though, son Mark and daughter-in-law Pam have stayed the closest to the Velcro family by not only hosting our gang over the years but by traveling with and assisting George in his travels after JoAnn's death. Here's Mark's take on their Velcro family experience.

Mark and Pam: Another Widmer Generation Heard From

I remember meeting Roy Lawson for the first time when I was in high school. I was on a trip to the East Coast with my parents and siblings and they took us to meet Roy and Joy when Roy was working as a professor at Milligan College. I was young, probably 15 or 16, and I thought it was really funny that this couple, who were friends with my parents, had names that rhymed. Roy and Joy, what a kick.

Roy seemed pretty old at the time, he must have been in his late twenties, and I do not remember much about this friend of my parents, except that he was small and seemed to be pretty important. Roy and Joy gave us a tour of the campus; it was quite impressive to a young high school student. Evidently it was not overly impressive, because I chose to study at Northwest Christian College, which just happened to be Roy's alma mater. It is also the college where Pam and I met and fell in love.

After the campus tour, I heard about Roy and Joy from my parents, but did not have a lot of contact until Pam and I started hosting members of the Lawson Velcro family in our home. We have probably been hosting for about ten years now, whenever the reunion has been held in Tillamook or

4. George's memory is not quite accurate, though I like his version better than mine. In 1955 I won a speech and essay contest during my junior year of high school, so I got to travel by Greyhound with 32 other high school students from Oregon, Washington, and British Columbia for a month's round trip to New York City. Our goal was to spend a week at the fairly new United Nations Building, learning about this international effort toward world peace. No, I didn't speak. But I listened eloquently!

5. Another slight correction. In high school I was president of Coast Christian Endeavor Union (from Newport to Astoria) and in college of Oregon Christian Endeavor Union. CE taught me the basics of leadership.

6. George's humility is one of his most endearing qualities. I think you can tell from his brief statement why he has always been so popular in the Velcro family.

Sunriver. We often hosted Kim and Ed, or Rich and Patti and their friends and children, and other special guests. This last year, we got to host Kim, Kyle, Nick, and McKenna, and Patti along with her granddaughter, Reyne. It has always been a pleasure to host the family in our home. There is always room in the Widmer hotel for the Lawson family. We have also enjoyed sharing meals and campfire time at the Jacob campground.

Mark and Pam

Last year, it was nice to hear about how many people in the group had been directly affected by Roy's ministry. Most people in the Velcro family probably are not aware that Roy took part in my ordination also. Roy spoke at my mother's memorial service, although we had to tape his message and play it at the service because he had other commitments.[7] He was able to lead her graveside service, and our family is eternally grateful. It was nice to

---

7. Yes. We'd flown to Oregon from Melbourne, Australia. We extended our stay and postponed our return flight because JoAnn, a deceptively tough little lady with an iron will, kept on living. We'd hurried from Australia because she was deemed to be dying any moment now. But she lingered in the embrace of this loving Widmer family. Who would want to leave them? Before Joy and I flew back I was able to conduct the graveside service for her but, as Mark said, couldn't stay for the larger memorial service. I felt honored to be able to participate.

sit with Mother and Roy and let her choose the elements of her service and the meal afterwards. No mystery meat sandwiches, she wanted the meal catered so no one would feel obligated to prepare food. She was so caring to the very end of this earthly life. It was so kind of Roy and Joy to interrupt their travel schedule to come back and share with us at that precious time.

One of my favorite campfire stories might not have taken place at the campfire. When Mike and Brian came to Sunriver for the Velcro reunion, Brian was following his GPS and driving through the Sunriver property. The roads seemed really narrow and it was not until later that he realized he had been driving down the bike paths instead of the streets.

For Pam and me our favorite part of the Velcro family has been getting to know some wonderful people, hosting friends, listening to tall tales around the campfire, sharing meals, and visiting with fellow Christians.

4

Other Tillamook Family

Brad and Gretchen Jacob

Brad, Gretchen, Lauren, Brenton, and (foreground) Katelyn, 2000

HERE'S ANOTHER EXCEPTION TO our "dysfunctional" rule. Brad and Gretchen just quietly eased themselves into the Velcro family. It started with their generosity. I think George Widmer is responsible. He invited us to have one of our earliest annual vacation weeks in Tillamook—then set about trying to find a place to host it. We'd already stayed at Cape Lookout, the state park at the ocean, due west of Tillamook. For that one George rounded up some RVs for us out-of-staters. The Jacobs dropped in on us there, their first exposure to our whole gang. (They got additional exposure when they and their children joined the group I led to the Holy Land a year or two later.)

I'm a little unclear how George persuaded Brad and Gretchen—knowing them, I doubt he had to apply any pressure—to let us take over their farm the first time, but I'm completely clear about how we then invaded their place again and again. They had an old farmhouse on the property, their former home. They lived there early in their marriage while Brad finished building their big house up the hill. They were sponsors for the church's youth group when they moved into their new house and out of the old one, so they simply told the church kids the house was theirs. They showed up every week for Bible study and hanging out. As long as the house stood, there were a couple of interior walls filled with their names and the dates. You could even find our grandkids' and great-grandkids' names there.

This, then, was the Velcro family annual vacation site for several years. Tents were pitched, trailers were parked on the grass, and the Jacobs' peace and quiet disappeared for a week.

Brad and Gretchen have never been *officially* dubbed "Velcro," because they come from functional families and they in turn have had a model one of their own, including Lauren and Katelyn and Brenton (and now their spouses and offspring). BUT, official or not, they are totally in the family and we wouldn't be without them.

Their generosity eventually rose up to bite them, though. Several times while Joy and I were "on the loose" we returned to Tillamook; every time we took advantage of the Jacob hospitality, usually staying with them in the big house up the hill. Then in 2019 we put on the full court press. I wrote Gretchen from somewhere asking for her help as a realtor. We were trying to locate an Airbnb in Tillamook, where we'd like to spend the summer before leaving the country for one last round of traveling. Turns out such rentals are practically nonexistent in our small hometown. Then she threw out, probably tentatively at first, this possibility: Would we like to stay in the empty farmhouse? Brenton and Brandy (and after a while their little son Rafe) had lived there for seven years, but they had recently bought a house in town, and this one now stood vacant. We must have surprised Gretchen when we jumped at the chance. We squatters happily spent the whole summer of 2019 there. We were in the house when the annual family vacation returned to the farm in July. We were there until October, when we left for our Grand Hurrah, the final extravagant trip around the globe before we would settle down permanently—in Tillamook, we thought at the time.

We probably shocked and maybe dismayed them when we asked (I hope we asked and didn't just announce) that if it was okay with them, we'd like to return to the old house when we came back to settle down in the States in February. When he retires Brad's planning to tear the house down and replace it with the retirement home he'll build for them. Probably our taking over the house as squatters encouraged him to proceed with these plans as soon as possible. (It's difficult to get squatters to leave; they think they have "rights," you know).[1]

Oh, there's another wedding involved, too. I got to marry Lauren Jacob and John Bruene—in the new barn Brad built for the occasion (yes, he had other purposes for it as well, but his deadline was to have the building up and operable in time for their ceremony. He met the goal.) It was not my easiest wedding. I had to compete for attention with a horse that kept poking its nose through the open door at the end of the barn. You can count on it. When a preacher and a horse compete, the horse wins. Every time.

It was a successful wedding. John and Lauren now have three children, Emma, Coy, and Dale. We can't get enough of them!

Brenton and Brandy Jacob have a son, Rafe. We get to see them from time to time, although not often enough to satisfy us. Brandy completed her doctorate in occupational therapy and is on the staff of the Adventist Hospital in Tillamook. Brenton works with his dad in construction. I think if they could afford it, though, Brenton and Brandy would be full-time surfers!

Katelyn and her husband, Wil Roberts, moved from Tillamook a few years ago. They now live in Lakeview, Oregon, where they are so happy it sounds as if they've abandoned Tillamook for good. Hard to imagine. Lakeview, you see, is pretty dry and sunny. Tillamook, on the other hand

---

1. The Scottish poet Robert Burns warns that the best laid plans of mice and men go oft astray. While Joy and I were in Africa over Christmas 2019, word went forth from Tillamook: The Lawsons are being evicted! See, I told you they would have to employ desperate measures to get us off the farm. It's good news, though. The Bruenes have sold their house and will move into the big house on the hill. Brad had to get rolling on building the Jacob's retirement home—which meant our squatter's mansion had to be razed. So by mid-February, we were outta there.

. . . Their infant daughter, Ciara, guarantees that grandparents Brad and Gretchen make regular trips south. They do their best to be there for all her important occasions. We get the reports.

Brad's Take on the Velcro Family

Our first introduction to the Lawson-Terrill clan was in 1999. Gretchen and I were invited to the bonfire at Cape Lookout State Park. We rode with Jon and Beth Cummings[2], and George and JoAnn were there also. The highlight was when Jeff pulled the homeless bum act.[3]

Later that year we were invited to go to Israel, Germany, and Austria on the Lawson-led Holy Land tour in 2000. Jon and Beth were also invited and so we went. It was during the first weeks of September and school for our kids. But we thought it would be a great trip for them, so they went as well.[4]

We learned so much and got to know more of the family. So many great memories of our time spent there.

From that point we had invited the group to come to our farm for the annual summer family vacation. I think we hosted six or seven years. We all have so many good memories. I think the bonfire times are my most memorable.

We also traveled to LaPine to Derek's a couple years and went to Cody, Wyoming for family vacations.

We have truly been blessed to be a part of this family. It has been so good to see the kids now becoming adults and growing their families and relationships.

---

2 Beth is George and JoAnn Widmer's daughter; she and Jon have been quietly in the background on many of our Velcro family outings. Dates haven't always worked for them; we want all of their company we can get.

3. It was dark. The only light was the campfire. Suddenly a very scruffy-looking stranger, long-haired and buck-toothed and obviously out of place, appeared in our midst. Scary. Until we finally recognized it was Jeff behind the disguise. He actually makes a pretty good bum.

4. This book has highlighted our annual vacation as a great opportunity for bonding with one another. Traveling together as we did on this Holy Land trip was another. The rest of us all fell in love with Lauren, Katelyn, and Brenton Jacob on this tour.

Aunt Faye and Lorraine Filby

Aunt Faye Filby and her sister, Lorraine, have belonged to the Velcro family almost from the beginning. Faye's and my careers have intertwined since she was a high school volunteer leader in children's church in Tillamook and I was one of the (. . . I almost wrote "brats" but realized Faye would never use the word even if she identified with the sentiment . . .) hyperactive children she tried to corral every Sunday. Then she left me behind to grow up when she went off to Northwest Christian College.

When I graduated from Tillamook High School, I also became a student at NCC. During my sophomore and junior years, I commuted from Eugene to the St. Johns Christian Church in Portland, where I'd become the youth minister. For years I embarrassed Faye if she was in any audience I was speaking for. I'd introduce her and tell the people that she and I used to live together. It was the truth, although not quite what it sounded like. We both lived with Bill and Liz Bish in their large home in the St. Johns district. She occupied the upstairs apartment. I slept in a bedroom on the main floor. She was Pastor Jess Johnson's full-time secretary; I was just a weekend warrior with the youth groups.

That's only the beginning, though. When I joined the faculty of Milligan College in Tennessee in 1965, Faye was already in Johnson City, once again serving Jess Johnson (he'd been our boss at St. Johns Christian Church and before that our pastor at our home church in Tillamook). Then when Jess moved on to Milligan College first as executive vice president and then as president, he once again summoned Faye to help him. After that overlapping period in Tennessee we went our separate ways, the Lawsons leaving Tennessee for Indiana and Faye returning to Oregon and then on to California.

But that's not the end of our connection. After I had been president of Hope International University in Fullerton, California for several years, I needed a new administrative assistant. Guess where I turned? I asked Faye, who was nearing retirement from her work with University Christian Church in Los Angeles, if she would like one more assignment before hanging it up. She accepted, so once again we were working together. After giving me three years, she returned to Oregon permanently, taking up residency in the Turner Retirement Homes.

Throughout all these years Faye's older sister Lorraine pursued her own career in Oregon as a dental assistant. And in her quiet way she slipped into our Velcro family along with Faye, coming with her to most family vacations when they were in Oregon. In their 90s now, they both still live in separate apartments in Turner. They can't make it to our family vacations now—Faye gave up driving a few years ago—but we haven't forgotten them.

5

Carole Boyd

Before We Learned to Think "Velcro"

TIGARD HIGH SCHOOL'S GIRLS' counselor summoned me to her office. I was in my second year as an English teacher there. Grace (after over half a century I've forgotten her last name) wanted to go over an earlier conversation, when the subject was the number of our students struggling in dysfunctional homes. I had mentioned, rather casually I suppose, that if she ever needed to place one of her charges in a home for a while, ours would be available. At this point Joy and I had been married just over three years. Our firstborn Kim was still a baby. Joy was also babysitting Big Jon, the newly adopted baby boy (such a hunk we were certain he'd grow up to be a football fullback) of the young French teacher on our faculty. So she already had her hands full, but we were young and idealistic and unafraid of a challenge.

That's how it happened. Carole, bright but troubled and at odds with her parents, became ours. I don't remember whether she had decided she couldn't live at home or her parents decided for her. There were all kinds of questions I didn't ask the counselor: How long would she be with us? Why couldn't she get along with her mother and stepfather? What exactly would be our responsibilities? She would be a ward of the court, which would cover some of Carole's expenses, but what else did we need to provide?

Just days after this conversation with the counselor our family consisted of Joy and me, baby Kim, and teenager Carole—and by day, Big Jon. We don't recommend "adopting" a teenager until you've had a little experience with your own children, but we didn't know that then. At first she fit right in. She was aware she really didn't have other options. And we loved having her with us. She quickly won Kim's heart. We still remember watching her play "So Big" with Kim, lifting the baby's hands above her head. Kim giggled with delight.

Carole turned sixteen when she was with us, old enough to take the test for her driver's license. Joy became her driving instructor; she believed—I don't know where she got the idea—that the man of the house might not have the necessary patience.

Carole's new license gave her increased independence, and that, as many another parent of teenagers can testify, led to some tensions. In time Carole decided that restrictions in the home she came from were easier to navigate than those we laid down, so she went back to her family. Mission accomplished!

Many years later, when Carole and her husband were living in San Diego and we were pastoring in Indiana, we drove with our whole family across the continent to attend the North American Christian Convention in Anaheim. While there we played hooky to spend the better part of a day with her and her three children, a son eight and twins, a boy and a girl, four. Several memories remain after all these years.

The first was the "Yes I mind if you smoke" button Carole wore that day. Trying to be polite, we swallowed our laughter, because we couldn't help remembering the several times she had assured us that of course she hadn't been smoking—though the smell of her bedroom and the butts on the outside window sill testified against her. We were glad, though, that as an adult she had kicked the habit.

The second was the lesson her twins taught me about the difference between parenting and grandparenting. Kim, Candy, and Lane did not hesitate to point out that difference. They couldn't believe what they were seeing. We were picnicking in a park between the car parking lot and the ocean. The grandfather's job was to be certain the grandchildren were out of danger from cars and water. Mostly, I just let them enjoy themselves at play while I enjoyed watching them. The stern disciplinarian was nowhere to be seen. "Who is this man?" our kids asked.[1]

---

1. Another memory has stayed with us from that same NACC week. The five of us skipped an afternoon session and headed for Huntington Beach. While the children played in the sand and surf and Mom was doing a little shopping, I sat by myself just casually surveying the landscape. That's when Kim came up and impertinently inquired, "Dad, are you bikini watching?" Now what's a father to do? Lie? Or admit that the

I've kept that lesson before me ever since. No wonder grandparents are more popular than parents who, especially when we are young, still believe we can "perfect" our children. We hold the reins too tightly and make far too many decisions for the children, wanting to protect them from danger and from the mistakes we made. For the best of reasons we retard their development and magnify their fears. We should simply enjoy them more.

Joy just reminded me of another fun memory. Carole came home one evening after going to a swimming party. She tried to shock us with her admission that she had been skinny dipping. We smiled and asked, "Did you like it?" It was fun seeing her startled look. Our underreaction was "one of our better moves," Joy recalls.

We haven't seen Carole since that reunion so many years ago. She had moved from Oregon to California, we from Oregon to Tennessee and then Indiana and Arizona. After a while we lost touch. We understood. She had successfully made her way through adolescence to adulthood and then parenthood. She had been reconciled with her family. We were a brief detour on her journey.

Carole lived with us for thirteen months. We didn't know it at the time, but she was preparing us for the Velcro family that lay in our future. Lessons she taught us?

1. We had made up our minds before she moved in that in "raising" a teenager, we should say *yes* unless we had to say *no*. She confirmed that this was the right decision. We'd take the same approach if we had it to do over again.

2. Every home has its own culture. Blending the two is never going to be easy. Carole's home, though religion was professed there, had a different set of standards from ours. Our practices seemed stricter, perhaps even more baffling, than those she came from. She conformed, but she was restless. We could have been more understanding.

3. As I said above, it's probably not such a good idea for new parents to jump into the role of parent to teenagers without having first gone through the phases between the cradle and puberty! We had a lot to learn. Carole taught us. We tried to remember these lessons as we approached our own kids' teen years.

---

landscape might have included some specific attractions of interest? I can't remember which I chose.

6

Jeff Terrill

Jeff and Joan with Kim and Kristin Terrill

THE WHOLE VELCRO FAMILY experience began with Jeff, although we didn't realize it at the time. We met when I was a twenty-four-year-old pastor (he probably guessed I was about 55) and he was a sixteen-year-old juvenile delinquent. Literally.

One Sunday morning in 1962 a pleasant, middle-aged woman showed up for Villa Ridge Christian Church's worship service. I had planted the church in 1959; it was still a very small congregation, probably fifty or sixty in attendance. You couldn't just drop in unnoticed. During the announcement period I welcomed her as I did every visitor. I didn't scare her—as we learned later, this woman didn't scare easily. Next Sunday she came back, this time with her son in tow. Jeff was tall (about six foot, four inches), dark, and handsome. Literally. He was also not at all pleased to be in church. Especially not pleased to be dragged there by his mother.

I called in their home that week, as was my custom. (Visitors were precious. We didn't let go of them if we could help it.) It was in their living room that I learned his story.

His mother had come to our church out of desperation. She was single, though she'd been married five times. She was at her wit's end. Jeff was spinning out of control. Just before she brought him to church he had been released from juvenile delinquent detention home—jail. He was there for stealing liquor from the Episcopalian vicar's garage. He was running with a pretty fast crowd. She was afraid she was losing him.

And there was something else. We didn't learn until many years later that Jeff was already an alcoholic, following in his birth father's footsteps. As I said, his mother was desperate, desperate enough to try church, about which she knew nothing. She didn't have the most basic understanding. She didn't know the Bible had two major divisions, Old Testament and New Testament. She might not have ever been in church before. And here she was, checking out this tiny congregation in its hand-me-down building (we bought it from the Baptists when they moved into their new much larger facility) with its green-as-grass minister. I still marvel that she didn't cut and run that first Sunday.

I can't really explain how and why Jeff and I bonded so quickly. Joy thinks it had something to do with my sermon his first morning. In the course of it I grumbled at some length about the popular Miss America Pageant, which had been televised that week. I made it clear that I didn't approve of its display of female flesh, the crassness of it all, the playing to men's weaknesses. I also confessed that I had watched it (strictly to get sermon material, you understand). Jeff decided on the spot, Joy believes, that this old man must not be totally out of touch with the real world. So he granted me a listen.

On my next visit to their home, I took Joy with me. She and Lillian, Jeff's mother, also quickly—and unexpectedly—bonded. I could not have predicted the deep friendship that ensued. Joy was only twenty-one, a small-town girl in the city, a quiet introvert married to a noisy little man. When she became pregnant, Lillian commented on how beautiful pregnancy made her; she "glowed," she said. And she was right!

If their burgeoning friendship was surprising, Jeff's and mine was astonishing. Jeff's interests were cars and girls and partying. He was not much interested in high school except for the hands-on classes like automotive mechanics. He was a student in two schools: Wilson High School in the morning for his academic subjects, Benson High School in the afternoon, where the curriculum offered classes for students who were definitely *not* in pursuit of traditional book learning. Even at Benson, though, Jeff ran into trouble. I, on the other hand, was then what I've always been: bookish, nonathletic, not-quite-in-step, and without a touch of mechanical aptitude. (Many years later our teenagers were flipping through my high school annuals. "Dad," they concluded, "You really were a nerd, weren't you?" Yes, I really was—am!)

But somehow we clicked. From the beginning I took pride in Jeff's abilities, especially his automotive aptitude. The Lawsons drove a respectable, dull 1955 Plymouth sedan. Jeff completely rewired it. I was amazed, first of all, that he *wanted* to do it for us as a part of his schooling and, secondly, that he *could*.

Among my fondest memories from this period were the times Jeff took me waterskiing. He was the teacher, I the pretty inept student. Still, he succeeded in getting me up out of the water, a new aptitude that served me well in our Arizona years, where I could join in the popular sport with the young people (and older) in our church. Jeff never lost his interest in water sports; over the years his toys included water skis, Jet Skis, several boats—all fast enough to pull a skier or two—inflatable kayaks, and whatever else was needed for a good time on or near the water. Once our annual vacations began, we made a priority of going where we could play in a river or lake. Using Jeff's toys, of course.

In this as in many other ways, Jeff assumed an increasingly large role in the Velcro family as his own family grew. He was our "firstborn" Velcro son.

But that was still in the future. The story he and I both often repeat has to do with what it took to keep him from another stint in jail as a teenager. I no longer remember what precipitated the crisis;[1] what I can't forget is Jeff's appeal: Would I help him talk his mother into letting him drop out of high school and join the Navy? I don't think he realized then what he was

---

1. But Jeff does. See his version of the story on page 48.

asking. I was pastor of Villa Ridge Christian Church, I was working on my master's degree at Reed College, and I was a teacher at Tigard Union High School. In other words, I was totally immersed in education. I was a true believer! And this restless, *brilliant* teenager was asking me to endorse his dropping out of high school.

I did it. Lillian had come to our church in the first place because she was desperate. She wanted to save her son from himself. Now it was my turn. I was afraid that if we forced Jeff to buckle under the weight of more schooling, he would get into even more trouble. By then I was persuaded Jeff had the intelligence and natural aptitude that he could excel in whatever field he chose. I hated to see him place his future in jeopardy—but that's what he would do if we insisted that he stay in school. If high school would even have him! So the Navy it was.

He didn't last long, but that wasn't his fault. After Jeff went into the Navy, the following September our family left Oregon for my new teaching job at Milligan College in Tennessee. We had only barely settled in—in fact it was during orientation week for new students—when Lillian telephoned with bad news. She had just received the results of her tests: cancer. The prognosis was bleak. We were devastated. This warm, loving, vibrant woman, who had become Joy's model and inspiration as mother and culinary expert and artist, was being taken from us.

Jeff's loss was much greater, of course. He arranged a transfer to Portland's Swan Island and then a hardship discharge so he could get home to take care of her. She died the next summer. Joy was in Oregon (I was studying at Vanderbilt) with our little daughters, so she was able to attend the funeral and be near Jeff. He gave her his mother's antique platform rocking chair, the one I always headed for when in their home. We enjoyed it for decades until, belatedly agreeing that Jeff should have it—after he mentioned one Christmas that he didn't have any of his mother's treasures—we gave it back. It's in "our" bedroom in the Terrill's home—where I usually sit for at least a little while whenever we stay with them.

After Lillian died Jeff went into a tailspin, as he tells it. He was working, wooing, and soon marrying Joan Pringle. It wasn't long before Shawn, Kim, and Kristin were added to the family. These are the bright spots of those years. But unknown to us, Jeff was drinking. Always resourceful, though, he managed his job and family obligations for a long time. He did his drinking away from home. The kids didn't know.

The Terrills remained in Oregon while the Lawsons were in Tennessee. Then we moved on to Indiana and from there on to Arizona and California. For many years the miles kept us apart. We were separated, but not divorced. Whenever we vacationed in Oregon we reconnected; when Jeff's work travels brought him near us, he visited.

There's much more to tell you about Jeff and Joan, but it'll come later, when I explain how our annual all-family vacation week began and when Jeff tells his version of the story. Without the Terrills' pivotal role, you understand, this Velcro family would never have been born.

Jeff and I have played this surrogate father-and-son role for fifty-eight years now. Though we use the language, our relationship I suppose is more easily understood by outsiders as friend-friend. But frankly that doesn't cover it. We've invested too heavily in each other for either of us to be able to say, "Here's my friend . . ." He's *more* than my friend.

Jeff's Side of the Story

I was born in Portland while living in Seaside, Oregon, in 1946 to a flamboyant mother and alcoholic father. They divorced when I was in the first, maybe the second grade. I was shuffled around Portland with friends and relatives for a couple years as Mom either worked the kinks out of, or into, her life. The next time I lived with her fulltime was as I entered the third grade after moving to Los Angeles. More about this later.

It was fifty-nine years ago, in 1961, when I was fifteen years old and in trouble from morning till night. Example: During that fifteenth year, a friend took his uncle's '55 Chevy pickup truck out for a joy ride. After I sneaked out of my bedroom, he picked me up a little after midnight. We didn't go two blocks before I knew we were in trouble. He didn't know how to drive! I told him to let me drive, but he refused until he rolled the truck on Garden Home Road. I drove it back to his house with no windshield and walked home. In the pouring rain. I had to pay half the cost of repairing the damage using my income of near nothing. I think my financially broke grandpa kicked in a little.

My poor mom was at a loss to know what to do with me. A year later, after I got my driver's license and a car, it got worse. Much worse. I skipped more high school than I attended. If not skipping, I was suspended for some little trick. Like in woodshop, when I squirted Elmer's Glue from a ketchup bottle down the back of a guy's pants because I thought he wore them too low.

I liked all things mechanical and transferred half my junior and senior classes to Benson Tech. I often "got lost" on my way across town with three other guys from Wilson, our academic high school. There were many times that we found ourselves at the beach, or Mount Hood, or out with my boat. By now I understood a bit about cars and woodworking. Along with my grandpa, we built a ski boat that, given enough time, would pull me out of the water. Water skiing was an activity I really enjoyed. But trouble was still calling my name.

Trouble . . . Like going with a neighbor kid into an Episcopalian vicar's home and swiping a fifth of gin. (Yes, I know, a vicar, which is a point Roy pounces on when he tells the story.) In the daylight. In front of his neighbors. In the neighborhood where we lived. The vicar pressed charges. I was arrested and locked up in Portland's juvenile detention home. Or as I called the place, jail. I was ashamed, mortified in fact. And frightened of the seriously bad guys locked up with me. *Big* bad guys.

The first day there I asked for a pad of paper and a pen and isolated myself on the far side of the grounds. A big guy dropped by to ask what I was doing. I told him the first thing that came to mind. I was undercover, collecting material for a piece I was writing for the *Oregonian* newspaper. He asked if I was going to mention him in my story. I said sure, if he'd leave me alone and not tell anyone what I was doing, right? Wrong. He told everyone and I had guys dropping by the rest of my three days in jail. But those guys that scared the willies out of me treated me like royalty instead of the hard time they gave other young or new guys. Because of a pad and pencil, I didn't have to fear them. I've wondered how long they read the newspaper before giving up on finding themselves in it.

One sunny Sunday morning during my junior year, and not long after my vacation in jail, I was in the driveway working on my car, out of trouble, minding my own business. Suddenly my mom popped up, grabbed me by the ear and dragged me to her car. Off we went, but to where I couldn't imagine.

What happened next was beyond my comprehension. We were sitting in front of a teeny-weeny little church building.

A church was the last place I expected to find Mom or me, no matter what was going on in our lives. My mom was a "colorful personality," to put it kindly. She and I lived for five years in the Los Angeles Basin where she either lived with or married several men—five as I recall, but maybe more. Our addresses usually ended with a half-number (as in 505½NE 8th) because we rented little run-down hovels in people's back yards. This was very popular in the 1950s in SoCal. I started the third grade there and left the end of the seventh. I changed schools often, sometimes two or three times a year, because we couldn't pay our rent and were evicted. Mom worked but didn't make enough to go around. I was left to my own devices after school and summers, and man, did I have a blast! I could write a book about the things I did and the trouble it caused, and even more about the trouble I *should* have been in but evaded.

But let me tell you this: I loved my mom to death, literally, as it turned out. And she loved me the same. There was never any doubt I was loved deeply, and I was very happy to live under her roof. She was a very special lady!

So here we sat in the front of this church, basically an old house without interior walls and with a few pews. She said, "We're going in." "Huh?" I said, stunned. But with my ear still hurting, in we went and sat down among maybe fifty or sixty people. Soon this geeky little preacher in horn-rimmed glasses walked in. Teeny-weeny, just like the building—he could hardly see over his pulpit! *This should be interesting*, I thought. He asked Mom and me to stand and introduce ourselves. Be careful when we sit back down, he said, because the pews can pinch. Ain't this just wonderful! Then he launched into what I supposed was a sermon. Somehow, he worked watching the Miss America pageant the night before into his message, and how he especially liked the swimsuit competition[2]. Another "Huh?" and I sat up a little straighter.

A few days later, Roy called on our home where we lived in an apple orchard. We had made our own cider, so we offered him a glass. By mistake Mom grabbed a jug that had gone "hard." We had a glass too, and after the first sip, we were aghast. Roy thought it was great fun. Little did we know then how hard it is to offend Roy. Unexplainably, during the next months Roy and I became very close. I remember the day it went from Roy-the-Preacher and Jeff-the-screw-up to something that fifty-eight years later, still can't be described. But let me tell you about that day.

Roy knew I had built a boat and liked to water ski. One day he mentioned he'd always wanted to learn how to ski. I asked him if he would like to go out with me and maybe I could teach him. To my surprise, he said

---

2. This is not at all how I remember it.

yes. What was I thinking? What was *he* thinking? My offer was meant to be a polite gesture. I never expected him to take me up on it, but he did! I was sixteen. Roy was an old dude, maybe twenty-four. How did I get myself into this, spending a day on the river with someone nearly twice my age? (Yeah, I wasn't much good at math.) But with lunches packed, we headed to the river one bright warm day, with me still wondering what I'd done. I drug Roy up and down the river for a long, long time. He eventually figured it out and skipped along like a little water bug, hunched over and legs out wide. But he skied a good distance before tiring.

When I pulled him into the boat, he looked exhausted. But it was hot out there in the sun, so I asked if he'd pull me. He agreed. I told him the one thing he needed to know about my boat and its outboard motor. "*Do not shut the motor off. Very important!*" I explained that the boat was built on a shoestring. The twenty-five horsepower Johnson Sea Horse that I could afford was worn out. That's why I could afford it! The motor was a two-stroke design and would start fine when cold, when the crankcase had contracted and the crankcase seals were doing their job. If turned off when warm, when castings had expanded and the seals were far from where they needed to be, the motor wouldn't run again until it cooled down. I explained all this to Roy, even that cool down took about three hours.

After skiing awhile, I got tired and dropped off. Roy circled around and when he came close, turned the motor off! I crawled onto the boat and don't really remember what I said. Probably nothing, but I remember what I was thinking! We got out our lunches and drifted down the river. FOR THREE HOURS! A messed up skinny kid's worst nightmare is to be stranded with an elderly, learned educator/preacher. I would have to answer this old guy's questions for almost an eternity. I was in deep water in more ways than one.

But you know Roy. I was quickly disarmed, we shared our stories, and by the time the motor would start, I wished it wouldn't. I came off the river that day hoping this guy was for real but fearful he wasn't, because no man had yet filled that hole for me. Why Roy cared about me was a mystery to me then and to some extent, still is half a century later.

If asked to pinpoint exactly when and where our Velcro Family started, it was that day. On the river. With a boat motor that wouldn't take me home. And a man who did!

A few weeks later, Mom and I accepted Christ, and Roy baptized us at the Lake Grove Christian Church. I was all in for Jesus and Roy, and I couldn't get enough of both. I found real friends in a high school youth group and hung out with the "good" kids. Yep, there's a first time for everything. With a good word from Roy, I got a job pumping gas for Albaugh's Mobile Station at SW Forty-fifth and Garden Home Road. School was still a problem because for me, the academic classes were a terrible waste of time. I just couldn't imagine where or how I could ever use the stuff they were selling. The shop classes at Benson, the technical high school, were another story, and I excelled there. Until a day that changed the course of my life.

Well into my senior year, I was taking an engine overhaul class. The school had a bunch of metal coffee cans that we used for collecting nuts and bolts as we dismantled motors. On The Day, I had my head under the hood of a car when a buddy with whom I scuffled, but only in fun, walked by with an empty coffee can, held it up to my ear, and rapped on the bottom of the can with a hammer. I jumped, hitting my head on the hood. It hurt. I told my friend if he did that again, I would knock him on his . . . can.

The teacher, a prickly little fellow with a rotten sense of humor, heard this. When I went back to work, he came by with an empty can, put it behind my head and hit it. I came boiling out from under the hood and, thinking it was my friend, hit the teacher between the running lights. Hard. On his way down, he shouted at me to head for the principal's office and he'd be right behind me.

I started in that direction but then stopped and thought it through. Bottom line: I was going to lose this one and I hated school anyway—all of it! I reversed direction, got in my car and went to the old Portland Pioneer Post office where all the branches of the military had recruiting offices. I tried the Air Force first, but they couldn't take me for ninety days. The Army was about the same. The Marines could take me in a month. I don't think I tried the Coast Guard. But the Air Wing of the Navy met me with arms wide open.

There was just one problem. I was seventeen and needed parental permission to enlist. Well now, I thought, this WAS a problem, one I doubted I could overcome with Mom. I went to Roy, explained the situation, and asked him to help me convince my mom to sign her approval. I'll never know if she was happy to get rid of me or if Roy had to persuade her, but she signed, and three days later I was on a plane headed to the Great Lakes Training Center in Illinois. (Isn't it interesting how Dr. Lawson, the great educator helped a kid drop out of high school?)[3]

3. It's even worse. Years later, when Jeff was the head of campus maintenance at Hope

I tried church while there. Once. It was dry, boring, ritualistic, and as far from my little Villa Ridge as I was from my home. I was very homesick. It took ten years before I went to church again on a regular basis.

I kicked around for the next ten years. While still in the Navy and on a shakedown cruise on the aircraft carrier *USS Constellation*, Mom contacted me to say she had leukemia, probably terminal. I asked for and was granted a hardship discharge to return home and care for her as she wound down. I worked a couple of jobs to make ends meet, but they didn't meet. I poked around at various jobs and after she died, drank nearly everything I earned.

Not long before Mom was found to be ill, I asked a girl named Joan out "for a Coke," as was the custom in those days when you didn't really know each other. She was a kid I had fond memories of from high school when we occasionally triple dated. Of course, not with each other. She was always kind to me. Somewhat to my surprise, she accepted, and we went to a café for those Cokes. We talked, and I was smitten. Mom was still alive when this occurred and when I got home that night, I told her I would marry Joan one day. Mom died a few months later. Joan and I were off and on for a couple years, but we eventually eloped in September of 1967. I was working as a grease monkey for a local machinery dealer. Not long after marrying, Multnomah County made me sell our house to cover the county hospital bills Mom ran up. We didn't have health insurance when Mom became sick and I had to put her in the county hospital, a terrible place to live out her last days! I regret all of it to this day.

In 1969 I caught the eye of a huge machinery dealer and surprisingly, I went from grease monkey to wearing three-piece suits and driving a new car, a '69 Pontiac LeMans. Our income soon doubled, tripled, then quadrupled. I was on commission, traveled extensively, and entertained heavily. And I thought more and more about Roy and that day on the river when I told him my story and he didn't cringe. I wondered if he'd cringe then if he knew I was living such a worldly life!

One time as I was traveling across the country, I stopped off in Indianapolis to see the Lawsons. It had been years since we were last together. I was ashamed because of my alcoholism, which at that time I had not admitted to myself. I was terribly apprehensive about my visit. I worried that I

International University, he honored a request from the head of chapel to speak to the students one day and be certain to give his testimony. Jeff hates public speaking, so I was surprised when he said yes. I was also pleased—until in his opening remarks he said he thought the Hope students deserved to know that their president had helped him drop out of high school. It didn't have to be said.

was overstepping a relationship I might only have imagined. However, it took but a few minutes for us to reconnect. It was as if we'd seen each other a week ago.

I remember Candy, age not much, climbing up beside me on a sofa, wiggling under my arm and just sitting there beside me. Talk about smitten! And I saw Kimberly and remembered when she was a few weeks old and brought her mom and dad to see Mom and me. I got to hold her when she was just a little baby. That was my first experience with being smitten by Lawson offspring. In fact, we named our first daughter "Kim" after Kimberly (Yes, Roy, Kim, not Kimberly!)[4]. There were a few other times when Roy and I connected, either in Oregon or wherever Roy was living at the time. I remember spending a day on the river with Roy and our boys and how perfect it all seemed. And we grew even closer.

Roy came to our home on occasion and we would catch up with him when he was in Portland to speak. I wanted our kids to know Roy and made it a point to associate them with Roy whenever possible. My son, Shawn, had just turned 16, had his driver's license, and I had just bought a new Porsche. Of course, the two of us took a road trip to Mesa that summer when Roy was at Central Christian. Shawn was a little guy, like Roy, and I wanted him to see that not all short men are crabby little people and that height is not the same as smallness. Roy is the perfect example of a big man who missed a growth spurt. Or two. Of course, he and Shawn got along great, and Shawn never considered himself small.

In the early 1970s Joan and our three children started attending the Canby Christian Church. It wasn't long before I started tagging along. I met Jay Hoffman, another preacher who is "real," and we became fast friends. In fact, we're close to this very day! But my drinking, which never occurred at home so my kids wouldn't have to see what I saw as a child, was killing me. I'm still not sure how much Roy knew or guessed. At the time, I hoped it was nil.

In 1985, three years after starting a machinery business, a successful one, I might add, I went to a treatment center for drug and alcohol addiction. It was grueling! Thirty days, twenty-four hours a day, a month-long ordeal that led me to understand why I drank and taught me how to get

---

4. OK, so I made a little mistake at Kim's wedding when leading the bride and groom through their vows. I asked Kim to repeat after me—you must understand: I knew she was named for our daughter but I didn't know she only got Kimberly's nickname—so I led her to say, "I, Kimberly, take you . . ." She abruptly stopped me. Out loud. Corrected me in front of everybody! "I'm *Kim*." So she is. And so much like her father!

sober and *want* to stay that way. It's been thirty-five years since my last drink, something I'm proud to share. Isn't it bizarre that at seventy-three, it still feels good to know Roy is proud of me too?

Also in 1985, Shawn asked if we could help his friend, Derek Hill, move back to Canby from Eugene where he had been attending the University of Oregon. We went, loaded his stuff in a trailer, and headed back up the freeway. As we neared Canby that evening, I asked Derek where we were taking him. He didn't have a clue, so we brought him home. And he stayed. About a year later he joined the Navy. After serving four years, he came home. And he stayed. It didn't take long for us to love each other. Good thing, too. By the time Derek returned from Navy we'd lost Shawn, we were in dire need of a son, and Kim and Kristin have a big brother again. He even took Kristin to one of her high school proms! Derek together with his boys, Jared and Reuben, enrich our lives far beyond what words can describe. He's one of our most cherished relationships.

We lost Shawn in July 1989. He was engaged to marry Toni on August 18. Roy blocked out time to perform their wedding. On July 21, a car turned in front of Shawn's motorcycle. He died lying on the road. I called Roy that fateful Saturday night to tell him his August 18 date had opened up and why. He said he had to preach the next day, including an evening service, but he'd be on a plane to Portland when he was finished Sunday evening. Toni and I met his redeye in the wee hours of Monday morning. Roy didn't just bury Shawn for us. He stayed with us for a week as he nudged my family back from the brink! He was a member of my family who truly cared. I should add that while Joan has a big family, I had none. My mom had been gone for years and my father, with whom I had no relationship, had also died. There was a half-brother, but I hadn't seen him in many years either. Roy was a lifeline that helped lead me back to sanity without a son.

Fast forward to 1994. Joan and I have taken our daughter, Kristin, and a friend to Camp Wi-Ne-Ma for a Memorial Day weekend campout. Saturday morning, there's a knock on the motor home door. I'm told Roy is on the phone, looking for me. How he thought to try Wi-Ne-Ma, I'll never know.

Our daughter, Kim, is attending Hope, and my heart sank because I expected Roy would tell me something awful had happened to her. Instead, he told me Lane, his son, had died the night before. It took a few seconds to switch gears from Kim to Lane and the terrible pit I knew Roy was calling me from. Finally, I asked where. Brookings, he said. What are you going to do from Mesa, I asked? Fly to Portland and drive to Brookings, says the little guy. Well, I said, go to our home when you land. We'll be there before you.

Roy rolls in with a rented minivan, very mini. When people started spilling out of the thing, I thought of those clown cars at the circus. There were Roy and Joy, Joy's mom and dad, Candy, Kimberly and Royce, and of course, Brian. In a mini, minivan for a six-hour ride down the Oregon coast. Holding suitcases on their laps, I guess.

As we sat in our family room, mostly in shock, I told Roy if he'd give me thirty minutes to get our motor home turned around and ready to go again, Joan and I would haul the whole clan wherever they wanted to go. Roy had to think it over—for about thirty seconds. We loaded up with snacks and toilet paper, lots of it, and off we went. It took a week to work through everything that had to be done.

As we were parting in Brookings, Roy and Joy heading to Fullerton and Joan and me to Portland, we started to talk about the tremendous time we had together surrounding the deaths of both our sons. Sure, there were tears. Lots of them. There was also much laughter. We really enjoyed being together, all of us. We decided then and there to vacation together for one week every year. No excuses, we promised each other. We'd do it. Some-where. This, we decided, would not only include our immediate families, but also those not of our own blood but just as close, whom Roy had collected along the way. It also included Derek, a man I knew as a messed-up kid I call a son today. You see, the only qualification needed to join our Velcro family is to be dysfunctional or married to someone who is. Except Mike!

Of course, I hear from Roy the familiar "you can work out the details." So, I did. The first year we went to Cultus Lake, high up in the Cascade Mountains of Oregon for an amazing week. There were maybe fifteen or twenty of us. Next it was to our home on fifteen acres, four miles south of Canby. Then back to Cultus where David, Roy's new son-in-law, sank my Jeep in fifteen feet of crystal-clear Cultus Lake water.

Since we started twenty-five years ago, we've been to the Holy Lands, Derek's ranch eight miles south of Canby, the Rondes in Colorado Springs, a Mexican Riviera Cruise for which Roy paid so he would have someone at his seventieth birthday party, Durango and Estes Park in Colorado, Millerton Lake near Fresno California (Why Fresno? It's a long story but everyone came!), Cape Lookout on the Oregon coast, and for several years, at our favorite camp, the Jacob's farm in Tillamook. This year, 2020, Roy is taking the whole clan on a one-week Caribbean cruise out of New Orleans for their sixtieth anniversary party! Last I heard there will be around sixty Velcro family members going, all with an amazing story of their own to tell.

Now you know when and where it all began and how our crazy, tearful, laughter-filled, over-the-top Velcro family vacations started. The many dysfunctional strays various of us have picked up along the way have their own amazing stories.

(So . . . Who thinks Roy turned that motor off on purpose?)

It seems only fitting that we should hear at this point from Jeff and Joan's daughters Kristin Terrill and Kim Woodring . . . and then from Kim's daughter to round out Jeff's story:

Kristin Terrell

Kristin Terrill

If my dad hadn't been so dysfunctional, then he never would have met you and Joy. You guys took an interest in him and welcomed him into your family. By doing so, you gave him a family that he didn't have, which means I got a family I never would have had. Your kindness set a good example for him, which he carried on by "adopting" Derek into our family. I am forever grateful.

Part 1: Meet Our Velcro Family

I've tried to explain our Velcro family to people over the years and I've learned that it's impossible to explain it in a way that they understand the full impact of what it's like to have such an amazing, extended, nonbiological family. Most people think I'm a little old to go on family vacations, and frankly think it's a little weird, but it's so much more than that. It's about connecting with people who have become your family through one way or another. It's the stories, the life experiences, and the relationships that bind us together. I've loved watching the way it's evolved over the years and wish I had kids to pass the tradition on to.

Kim Woodring

The Woodring Family

It has been a privilege to be a part of this Velcro family that has grown through loving one another during really hard times. Shawn's and Lane's deaths cemented the bond of love between the Terrills and Lawsons. It's a bond that won't be broken as long as future generations continue to feel the connection and love that brought us together.

It has been wonderful to watch others join the family over the years. My family is small. Dad is an only child and Mom's sister never married. Shawn died, and Kristin never married. We didn't grow up around cousins. And on my side of the family, my children Madi, Cade, and Joel have a relationship with only one second cousin (or third cousin or first cousin twice removed . . . I have no idea what it technically is) that they have a relationship with. So this large, wonderful, Velcro family has filled a void in my life.

I lived in Tennessee when Lane died and I remember my dad keeping me informed and in the loop as he set out on his journey to Brookings. I remember when everyone met up in Canby and Cultus Lake for the next gatherings. I wanted so badly to be a part of it, but it wasn't until 1997 in Colorado Springs that we got to join the Velcro family in the fun. I am truly thankful to the Lawsons and my parents for opening their families to one another so we could be a part of something bigger. And I don't just mean the size of our family. The love, acceptance, and care through hard times like death, divorce, and cancer is priceless. And so is the joy in weddings, births, new families, and new places.

Our Velcro family has a tradition of telling stories—the same stories and new ones year after year. This year was especially entertaining watching Eden as she got the jokes and was tickled about hearing the grandma story. Her reaction gives me hope that the young people will want to keep this alive. I know, Brian is tired of telling it but I'm afraid he's going to have to keep doing it.[5]

What makes us different is that Roy and my dad chose to be a family and extended that to the rest of us. They could have left it as a friendship, but they decided to create a place where we all belong and are loved. There's a sermon illustration in that, but I trust Roy to articulate it better than I can. I know the Velcro family is important to Madi, Cade, and Joel. They are in the stage where they are drifting away as they grow and get established, but I'm confident we will see them from time to time and they will be back with their families in the future. The cool thing about the Velcro great-grandkids and future generations is this is all they know. I think we will be surprised at how important this part of their family is to them.

5. I told you some of the stories had grown whiskers. Brian has been telling the grandma story as long as we've had campfires. In other words, from the first year we were together. It's too long to include here, and it requires his inimitable dramatic style, so I can't recount it. Let's just say he didn't mean to assault his friend's grandmother; it was a case of mistaken identity.

Part 1: Meet Our Velcro Family

Madi Johnson

Growing up, the Velcro family vacations were the highlight of my summer, if not my year. To be honest, I look forward to them more than I look forward to Christmas simply because I get to spend time with my family. The best memories of my life have come from family vacation, whether it be hunting salamanders with my cousins, sitting around the campfire listening to stories, or singing karaoke on the Mexican Riviera cruise. My Velcro family has given me my sense of humor and adventure, and they are the most fun people I have ever met. They challenge me to see the world in different ways, and are always there for me when I need them. The Velcro family vacations have been one of the most consistent things in my life and never disappoint me or let me down. They give me a glimpse of what Heaven will be like. I am always proud to tell people about this part of my life. I consider it an honor to introduce my friends to any one of my family members. I would not be who I am without them, I and hope to carry on this tradition for the rest of my life.

7

Tennessee 1965–1973

Sharman Bean

NOT ALL OUR STORIES end happily. I've already confessed we had a lot to learn when Carole lived with us. I've wondered whether, if we had been more mature ourselves, we could have built a lasting relationship with her. When we were together in San Diego for that brief visit we seemed to pick up where we had left off many years ago. We were happy to see her again. But then once more we drifted apart. We've often thought about her and wondered where she was, where we went wrong, how we could have stayed in touch. But she was in California and we were thousands of miles away. And in those days there was no Internet, no Facebook. Eventually our mutual busyness separated us.

Sharman's story is even more painful to relate. Her parents had been close friends since 1957, when I was youth minister of St. Johns Christian Church in Portland. It was a weekend ministry; I commuted from college in Eugene, about a three-hour drive in those days. During my two-year stint there, her parents, Howard and Vera, worked with me as sponsors to the junior high youth group. They had four little children of their own, so this was a substantial commitment. Vera, who later became one of Joy's best friends, was another of her inspirations as wife, mother, gardener, and cook *extraordinaire*. We both appreciated Howard: quiet, hardworking, faithful husband and father. I had grown up working in my father's grocery stores. Howard was also a grocer; we spoke the same language.

One day as I scurried up their sidewalk for a leaders' meeting in their home in St. Johns, I spotted the For Sale sign in the front lawn. I yanked it out of the ground, hauled it inside, and demanded to know what this nonsense was all about. I couldn't stand the thought that Howard and Vera would no longer be a part of our team. I protested in vain. Howard had bought a "Mom and Pop" store in Beaverton. At the time I had no idea I'd soon be moving to Tigard, Beaverton's next-door neighbor in southwest Portland, to plant Villa Ridge Christian Church.

Fortunately, not long after the new church was underway, they became stalwart workers in it. Howard in time served as an elder. Joy was my wife by this time, and, as I said, Vera soon filled many roles in her life. Howard did me another favor. We were always strapped for money–I was a poor preacher in more ways than one–and Howard hired me from time to time to give him a little relief in his store (and to ease our financial stress). He also occasionally sent me home with meat he couldn't sell. Joy considered this as mixed blessing, as sometimes the meat was a little more mature than she appreciated. She worked miracles repairing the evidence of age with generous coverings of Campbell's Cream of Mushroom soup.

We worked together in Villa Ridge and later Tigard Christian (after the church moved into its new building) for a few years. Then it was our turn to leave. The Lawsons moved to Tennessee; Howard and Vera and their four children remained in Oregon, and for a few years we had to be satisfied with occasional letters and our periodic vacations back to see friends and family there.

After three years on Milligan's faculty, I took a leave of absence and moved us from Johnson City to Nashville to complete my doctoral studies. It was a risky decision, since by this time we had three little children and I was going off salary. I had received a teaching fellowship from Vanderbilt University, but that wouldn't support a family of five. I patched together several part-time jobs, including one as music/worship minister at Eastwood Christian Church across town. The second year I added a job as manager of Morgan House, a ten-story high rise for married students, 120 apartments in all. I had the title, but Joy did much of the work (she scoured 85 ovens that year), although I did hire myself as garbage man. That paid a few more bills.

But that was the second year. For the first we had to make do with my fellowship stipend and the small check the church paid. We made it. Barely.

What I hadn't included in the calculations, because I didn't know I'd have to, was the cost of adding one more person to the family. This challenge presented itself shortly before we left Johnson City for Nashville, when a worried Vera phoned from Beaverton. They were in trouble. Their teenage daughter, who had been a challenge for her parents, was pregnant. She had just told them. She was still in high school. She was scared and so were they. This was the 1960s. The sexual revolution hadn't yet transformed America's attitude; nice girls didn't get pregnant. Abortion wasn't an alternative. Shame was the consequence.

So they asked, "Could Sharman come and live with you until the baby is born?" Of course we said yes, though we weren't quite sure how to make it work. We had already made arrangements for our housing. We'd found an apartment in what I flippantly referred to as "exclusive housing." You couldn't live there if you made much money. In other words, public housing. This was the South, which meant that most of our neighbors in the development were African Americans. One day our very blond daughter Candy stood on our door stoop and watched a little boy walk by. There was something different about him. He wasn't black like most of her playmates. "You're just a little white boy," she called to him. Reverse discrimination, I guess. Candy's usual playmates were black, so she was surprised to see "a little white boy" in the neighborhood.

There were five of us when I signed the rental agreement. Now we were six. It was tight, but we found room for all of us. It was also tight financially. Sharman's parents sent Sharman a check for fifty dollars each month, but that was spending money for her, not room and board money for us. (If they had known our financial situation, they would have arranged to help. But they didn't know, and we were too proud to tell them.)

We enjoyed Sharman's time with us. She was good with the children, helpful in the kitchen. She went to church with us, where the good people embraced her as part of our family. As her pregnancy progressed we began making plans. I used some of my contacts to arrange for a good family to adopt the baby. Joy went to the hospital with Sharman and played the absent father's role, holding her hand before the delivery and being there when Sharman recovered.[1]

---

1. A footnote about that baby. Many years later Joy and I were walking along a sidewalk at the North American Christian Convention in the Midwest when we spotted friends ahead. They had a small boy (no more than ten or twelve) with them. As soon as they recognized us, they brought the boy over. "These are the people who helped us get you," they told him.

Then still more years later I received a phone call from a young man (I think he was about 28 by then). He had learned again of our role in his life while going through his

Part 1: Meet Our Velcro Family

The next part of the story I still hate to relate. After the baby was born, Sharman, who had kept fast company in high school, reverted to her old ways. She found a crowd to party with, stayed out all hours, and forced a confrontation with us. I remember with deep regret when we met in my office at Morgan House, where we were now living. I told her we couldn't continue as things were going. "You want to be free of us," I said. "That works both ways," I added, implying that to be free in one direction means being free in both.

That was our last conversation. She moved on.

What did I learn from this? I learned—once more—that sometimes I just need to keep my mouth shut. Words cut. Sometimes they sever completely. I did speak the truth, but too harshly. Sharman demanded the right to do as she pleased. She took whatever was offered her during this critical period of her life but seemed to feel no sense of obligation to us for taking her in, to her parents for rescuing her when the future looked so bleak, or to the generous people who gave her son a good home and positive start in life. So, as I said, I spoke the truth. But how I wish I hadn't said it.

But there is—it gives me great pleasure to add—more to the story. After this book was published, I was finally able to locate Sharman again. We had a good conversation. I was concerned that I may have written too much, disclosing a closely held secret that she did not want told. I worried without cause. She told me she long ago had reconnected with her son. They haven't let go of each other since; even better, he and her other children are family. She also explained some health issues she has struggled with all her life, issues which go a long way toward accounting for her puzzling behavior back when she lived with us. In turn I let her know how proud we were that she chose to carry the baby instead of aborting his life and that she then loved him enough to give him to parents who could provide a good future for him.

I opened this chapter with these words, "Not all our stories end happily." But as you can see, I was premature. We hadn't yet learned the rest of the story. We had to wait awhile, but now I can write, "Here's a story that ends happily."

---

recently deceased father's papers with his mother. That's when he had decided he'd like to meet his birth mother. Could we help him locate her? We said we'd try. We didn't have contact information for Sharman, so we called her mother. She was unsure whether Sharman would welcome this meeting but said she'd check with her. Only a day or two passed before Vera called to say Sharman was willing, and she gave us her phone number, which we passed on to Sharman's son. We were then out of the picture, but we learned the meeting did in fact take place. It was, it seems, satisfactory, but the two never got together again.

8

Indiana 1973–1979

Carolyn Webster (Hollingsworth)

Jim and Carolyn Hollingsworth's wedding day 1984

CAROLYN'S STORY IS A happy one. It's more Joy's than mine. I was there at the beginning, but I pretty much retreated to the background as Joy and Carolyn became lifelong mother/daughter and friend/friend.

Part 1: Meet Our Velcro Family

At the time (1973-1979) I was pastor of East Thirty-Eighth Street Christian Church in Indianapolis. My secretary forwarded a phone call from Robert Webster, who lived in New Castle, Indiana, about an hour from the city. His younger sister was in the hospital in Indianapolis. Somehow he had heard of me. Would I be willing to call on her? She's pretty discouraged, he said, and could benefit from a pastor's call.

So Joy and I went. The young woman we met was a kindergarten teacher in the city system. I think she was in her fifth year of teaching in a difficult part of town. Her degree was in early childhood education; her principals overloaded her with special-needs children. Her resources were depleted: physically, she was sick; financially, she was broke; emotionally, she was depressed; spiritually, she had nothing left to draw on. We talked and I prayed and promised to see her again. Which I did.

It was November. Joy and I always tried to make holidays special at our house by inviting others to join us, often persons who would otherwise have been alone. Naturally we invited our new friend Carolyn. That was our first step toward becoming family. When her apartment was broken into, she had not yet recovered enough to weather another crisis on her own, so we invited her to stay with us for a few days. She stayed nine months.

She was a blessing. We were dealing with a crisis of our own. Our eleven-year-old daughter, Candy, was seriously ill. It wasn't epilepsy, though it acted like it. She was experiencing repeated convulsions and blackouts every day, cause unknown. Her doctor was baffled. She required constant attention, even needing hospitalization twice.

Fortunately for us, Carolyn loved and understood children. So here was a win-win: while she was regaining her strength in our home she was also attending to Candy's needs. Among other things, she tutored Candy, helping her to keep up with her classwork when for some weeks she couldn't go to school. And Carolyn did night duty. She later needled Joy and me because when we go to bed at night, we sleep rather soundly. Well, that's almost the truth: Joy sleeps soundly naturally. I've been half deaf since infancy; that's my excuse for not hearing a child's cry. So it was Carolyn who answered Candy's nighttime calls—and her younger brother Lane's, also, if he needed something.

Thanks to Bob Webster's phone call, Carolyn became a live-in nanny and tutor for the children, a friend in need for the children's parents, and in some ways another (adult) child for us. I mentioned that when we got acquainted, she was pretty well drained of resources. We could help

62

financially by providing a place for her to live (she was able to leave her apartment); physically, by offering a place to rest and recuperate; emotionally, we could "be there" for her; and spiritually, she could get rooted in our healthy church.

Life hadn't been easy for her. When she was twelve her father was killed in a railroad crossing accident. The marriage was strained before that. Carolyn was closer to her father and emotionally estranged from her mother. When he was ripped from her life, she felt at sea. From Joy she received the mothering she felt deprived of when she was younger. Joy loved her back to health. (Like Carole Boyd in Oregon years earlier, in time Carolyn also enjoyed a renewed and rewarding relationship with her mother.)

After a while she was ready to be on her own again, so she moved into her own apartment. But she never left our family. We eventually moved to Arizona, but distance didn't separate us. It was only natural, then, that when she met and married Jim Hollingsworth, she'd ask her surrogate father to do the honors. She was still teaching school at the time; Colonel Jim Hollingsworth was second in command with Indiana State Police. Finding time for the nuptials was a challenge. But they were able to make the arrangements, so in the appointed season (it was during Christmas holiday) they flew to Arizona where they were married in our living room.

Their story continues. When their son Jacob was born we quickly claimed him as our Velcro grandson. Not long ago I had the privilege of presiding at the wedding of Jacob and Elizabeth. As I write, Jacob is enjoying his flight training at Vance Air Force Base in Oklahoma, keenly anticipating his new career with the Air Force.

Son, Jacob Hollingsworth

Carolyn's Story—as told by Carolyn

This is Carolyn's story of our meeting and earliest experiences together. You'll notice that our two accounts differ at several points. Memory does play tricks on us. Since I'm considerably older than she is, I suspect hers is the more accurate telling. However, I like mine so well I've included both versions.

The first time I saw you was at Methodist Hospital. My brother had called the church and asked for someone to come see me. You were on your way out of town for a speaking engagement, so both you and Joy stopped at the hospital on your way. I promised to visit the church as soon as I got out of the hospital. So four days later I was at East Thirty-Eighth. I knew I needed to get back in church, so when the invitation hymn came, I made my way down front. I looked and felt weak so you had me remain seated. This was the Sunday before Thanksgiving. Then on Wednesday of that week I came home from school to find I had a break-in. All my electronics were taken. I called the apartment manager to get the door glass fixed, and he said he had no support staff to fix it until Monday. So I called the church to see if someone could help me. Roy and Mike Kouns showed up and boarded the door; then they invited me to Thanksgiving at the Lawsons.

I didn't sleep all night, so I went to your house to feel safe. I looked so bad but would not stay that night. You made me promise to come by the church Friday to see you. There you called Joy and told me to go to your house for a nap. I lay down for a nap, and then it was Saturday. Then I went home for the night and showed up Sunday at church tired again. After Sunday night church Joy talked me into staying at her house and went with me to the apartment to get my stuff.

That Monday after school you and Joy had a talk with me. You said you traveled a lot and it would be a help to Joy if I moved in. You offered to move your office to the church to make room for my bedroom furniture. The rest of my stuff we put in the garage. Some men from the church moved me.

That New Year's I was having ulcer problems and took too much Maalox. It clogged the urethra, and I damaged my bladder; thus after surgery to unclog it I had to catheterize myself for seven months. When it would fill up it would cause me to have a vagal nerve reaction and faint. Surgery was required, to be followed by seven months of catheterizing myself.

On the surgery date I called to talk to Joy, and you said she had gone out for groceries. My voice broke, and you told me she was coming to the hospital.

While I was living with you Candy had problems and I tutored her with materials Joy got from her teacher. We had her in the hospital with Dr. Miller, who figured her out. She was there over Christmas, and we took eight-hour shifts with her. Joy stayed days, then I stayed three to midnight, and Roy slept there. We got her home just as I got sick.

Later that winter the flu went around. Candy upchucked in her bed and all over herself. No one heard her but me. I cleaned her up with a warm bath and put her in my bed. Then I put her sheets in the wash and left her bed open to air out. Not one parent heard us.

The spring came, and we were doing better. The last day of school I resigned. As a result of my surgery, I was wearing a catheter, and I felt I was risking infection for myself in dirty public schools. When school let out we were preparing for a trip. Joy asked me to go to Heritage, the kids' Christian school, and pick up the kids' report cards. I told the lady I had just quit my teaching job. She told me they had openings, and Mr. Ralph Hayes was called to interview me. I was hired to teach kindergarten on the spot.

When I went with you from Indiana to Oregon you told the people at the convention where you were speaking that I was on a shopping trip for a man, that on the last verse of the altar call at Turner guys who wanted a good mate should come forward. I about died.[1] When we returned home I found an apartment with another teacher near you. Then in April you left the area.[2]

Other Indianapolis Stories

A couple other young people lived with us briefly in Indianapolis. I mention them as further evidence that there's no smooth, predictable pathway into a Velcro family. As I've already confessed, not everybody sticks.

Kelly Wilmoth was Kim's close friend in school. Kelly's minister father died at only thirty-six (my age at the time); her mother Eileen had to find

1. I'm afraid she's telling the truth, mostly. I was speaking at the Oregon Christian Convention held on the old convention grounds in Turner and I did introduce her, not at the "altar call" but in the introduction to the message. As you can tell, Carolyn hasn't forgiven me yet. Nor should she!

2. This is when we moved from Indianapolis to Mesa in 1979.

a job to support her children. She secured one with Standard Publishing Company in Cincinnati, Ohio, but Kelly wanted to finish the school year before moving from Indianapolis. Kim invited her to stay in our home for the remainder of the year. (You're going to see this pattern with Kim as our story goes on.) We'd have liked to keep Kelly, but her mother needed her in Cincinnati.

Toward the end of my first year as pastor of the church, a deacon recommended that an employee of his come to see the preacher for some counseling. Hap, single father of an irresistibly cute four-year-old daughter, was royally messing up. He was a successful salesman whose charisma—engaging smile, quick wit, good looks, winning way—knew no bounds. Neither, apparently, did his ethics, as I subsequently learned. I can't remember now what he had done. What I haven't forgotten, because it's the only time this happened to me in sixty years of ministry, is that he had only barely begun telling me his plight when the police knocked at my study door. They had traced him to church. I asked for a few more minutes alone with him; I needed to hear the rest of his story. Then they took him away.

After they left, I asked the church secretaries, "Does this happen often here?"

"Only since you got here," they replied.

I stayed in touch with Hap while he served his prison sentence in Lansing, Michigan. When he was released, I picked him up and brought him to move into our home; he could stay with us until he got back on his feet. He liked the idea so much he soon moved his four-year-old daughter in as well.

It didn't work out. Hap also liked the fast life too much to give it up. He regularly left his little girl in Joy's care, then partied to all hours. We caught on; we had become enablers. As I had invited him in I now had to invite him out. What hurt, though, was this meant giving up his little girl; we had all fallen in love with her. Hap, an accomplished con man, had demanded legal control of his daughter but didn't want to take care of her. He was "happy" to leave all the parenting chores to Joy. She was glad to do them, but we had to admit this arrangement wasn't beneficial for either of them.

You can see we were not quick learners as we were figuring out what it takes to become a Velcro family. In this instance I wish I had been more cautious and hadn't asked quite so much of the family. It's one thing for me to run the risks that are part of a pastor's calling; it's another thing to place one's wife and children in potential jeopardy.

9

Brian Matlock

Uncle Brian

WHEN DESCRIBING OUR VELCRO experience, the two stories I tell most
often are Jeff's and Brian's: Jeff's, for reasons you've already read, and
Brian's, because it's always fun to recount how he wormed his way into
the family. He's the most deliberate addition. There hasn't been any way
to get rid of him!

We moved from Indianapolis to Mesa in 1979. We had barely finished unpacking when Brian started hanging around. He was attracted to our daughter Kim, a high school sophomore; Brian was a year older. They dated a little. Not much, Kim insists. What I noticed was that even though they weren't dating, Brian was still under foot. I got up one morning to discover he had spent the night on the family room couch. "Brian," I asked with what I thought was evident sarcasm, "do you want to just move in?"

He did. He's been a part of the family ever since.

He was actually one of a larger gang of teenage boys who spent a lot of time at our house. Teenage daughters Kim and Candy attracted them "like flies," I groused. I especially remember Brian, Bruce, Kevin, and the two Marks, who typically appeared late afternoon or early evening, usually around mealtime. But Brian was the one who made himself at home the most often.

He definitely met the criteria for membership in our Velcro family—a team we hadn't adopted yet, but the outlines were beginning to take shape. Like Jeff's, Brian's parents had divorced. His mother was with her second husband, his father with his fourth wife. Both of his parents were well-educated professional people: she was a counselor and teacher, he a lawyer with a private practice in Mesa. Like Jeff's father, Brian's was also an alcoholic.

Brian's closest friends for years were—and still are—Bruce Kellogg and Kevin Carlson. In fact, shortly after our ministry in Mesa began, all of these guys were in Central's youth group, thanks to Kevin's influence. Kevin's and Mark Palich's families were longtime members; for Mark Rogge, Bruce Kellogg, and Brian, though, church was pretty new. When Kevin baptized Brian, he became the only professed Christian in his family. A few years later I got to preside over both young men's ordinations into the ministry.

Several times in recent years, decades after he joined the church and our family, Brian has given his testimony about what church did for him. His whole life was changed, he says, in ways he could never have anticipated as a teenager. He went to work as a leader in the children's department when he was still in the high school youth group. He learned to play the guitar so he could assist in youth meetings and children's church. He joined Salt of the Earth, the large youth choir that sang regularly in church services and on tour. They performed for the North American Christian Convention in Kansas City, Missouri, in 1982.

He blossomed. While studying science and mathematics at Arizona State University in next-door Tempe, he felt called to ministry. The church's former minister, Charles Cook, had left Mesa to become professor of practical theology at Manhattan (Kansas) Christian College. Brian and Kevin and Bruce followed him there. As a student Brian preached for a small church, then after graduation returned to Arizona to serve as an intern at Christ's Church of the Valley in Phoenix. Subsequently he became youth minister at Fountain Hills Christian Church.

Like his surrogate father, in time he became a vocational schizophrenic. For many years he combined his interest in real estate investing with his dedication to church ministry, succeeding in both. After Fountain Hills he became an associate minister of Central Christian, which meant we got to work together, although to avoid any hint of nepotism he never reported directly to me. He remained on the staff another year after I retired, then turned to real estate as his full-time occupation. He's remained active as a Central Christian Church volunteer ever since.

For more than forty years Brian has been at the heart of this family. At one point five teenagers lived with us: Kim, Candy and Lane, biological offspring; Rosa, our Ecuadoran exchange student (about whom more later); and Brian. Bedrooms were distributed as follows: Roy and Joy in one; Candy, Kim, and Rosa in their own; and Lane and Brian without one. They slept in the family room. Brian, because he was older, got the couch. Lane, because he was younger and more accommodating, got the floor behind the couch. Brian still tells about his morning ritual: He usually got up first. He'd stretch, climb over the couch—an unnecessary maneuver—so he could trample on Lane, his gentle way of rousing his younger adoptive brother.

That pretty much symbolizes Brian's role in the family. He moved in and brought laughter with him. His sharp wit and mischievous temperament were always on display. In time he became Uncle Brian to younger generations of Velcros up to and including this year's all-family vacation, when around the campfire every evening he read the ongoing saga that great granddaughter Eden, twelve, wrote each day. He not only read her compositions. He starred in them. Eden killed him off in almost every episode, but then she brought him back in the sequel so she could wipe him out again.

In the early years, when Brian was at our house almost every day but hadn't yet moved in, he found something that was missing in his own family at the time. He had two homes, one with his mother and step-father and the other with us. But his relationship with his stepfather was uneasy and the marriage had become troubled (and ended not many years later).

He loved his parents and they loved him and he knew it. Hanging out with our family wasn't a rejection of his own but more of a redefining of family--and his role in it. We're proud to report that we gradually saw the bonds with both his parents—and with his biological brother and sister—growing stronger. The Velcro family didn't replace his own but in a paradoxical way deepened his love for his birth family. It has been a win-win.

One more important part of the story should be reported here. Joy and I lived in Payson from 1988 to 1996. For most of our marriage Joy had struggled with her health. After testing the air in Payson—which at the time had a reputation for its pollution-free environment—we bought a house there. We made Payson our home until 1996, when Joy felt strong enough to move back to the Valley. By this time I was still serving as pastor of Central Christian in Mesa but had also become president of Pacific Christian College (to become Hope International University in 1997), so for several years I had a three-way commute including Payson, Mesa, and Fullerton, California. (My joke in those years was that every week, when I wasn't traveling elsewhere, I slept in three beds in two states with one woman!)

Our Arizona residency requirements (and costs) were eased when we and Brian agreed to build a house together just a couple of blocks from the church. He and Joy did most of the work—selecting the lot, designing the building, decorating the interior. Brian and I mostly yielded to Joy, since she's the interior designer—and she has the good taste. Brian helped with the logistics. As usual when Joy and I are involved in building or remodeling projects, I went to the bank.

It worked well. We lived together until 1999, when after twenty years I retired from the church and we moved full-time to California. Brian arranged for the sale of the house.

Brian's Story

In the Fall of 1979, my senior year of high school, my friend Kevin Carlson invited me to go to church with him. I guess such an invitation is not so unusual, and I doubt I considered it so at the time. High schoolers invite friends to churches, or baseball games, or to parties, and any number of other activities. But that simple invitation ended up triggering what would become one of the most meaningful chapters of my life.

That year I wandered into Central Christian Church, a congregation of 400–500 people. They had recently built a new auditorium which sat on a few acres of land in downtown Mesa, and had just hired this new preacher, a preacher that was nothing like what I thought a preacher was supposed to be. He lit up that auditorium with all kinds of enthusiasm, laughter, and excitement. His sermons gripped me. He said things that mattered to me, that inspired and challenged me. And that church was nothing like what I thought a church would be. It was full of deep, defining, revealing laughter. Maybe more importantly, it had an air of invitation—I quickly sensed that if I wanted in, they wanted me. I wanted in.

I didn't realize it at the time, but it was an electric time for that little church. Seeds of change were being planted by new leadership, and the groundwork for a huge vision was being laid, one that would roll out profoundly over the following decade. I became caught up in the excitement and forged dozens of new, deep friendships, many of which have stayed with me through today. Though I had no understanding of the depths of what was happening in that place *around* me, I very quickly realized that something profound was happening *to* me: This church and these people were changing me.

I became deeply involved in the youth programs. My teenage life was dominated by Wednesday-night choir practice and Bible study, Sunday school, summer camps, and choir tours. In that youth group I made friendships that have become the backbone of my life. I became close friends with Kim Lawson, Lisa Richeson (now Palich), Mark Palich, Mike Prior. My friendships with Kevin Carlson and Bruce Kellogg were already established, but they became *lifelong* friendships at Central Christian Church.

Kim, who happened to be the preacher's daughter, invited me home a couple times where I got to meet her family. I suspect she and her family sensed some signal of what I was experiencing. The time inside the Lawson home revealed to me a strange longing I didn't realize I had: to be part of a family that watched television together, did jigsaw puzzles, recollected the day's events at dinner, and sang in the car. Most of my peers were trying to escape such a routine, but I found it irresistible. I was hooked.

My parents divorced when I was five. Though I had grown up with my dad living not far from me and making every effort to stay connected to his son, my bond to him steadily decayed through my middle and high school years. I'm ashamed to say I didn't make much effort to be in touch. Our values and beliefs differed substantially, and the lifestyle I was choosing through the church was tremendously different than the one my dad lived. Though he loved me and I believed he was fundamentally a good man, his was a life lived in bars, with an active rotation of women, and he carried a deep suspicion of religion. We weren't estranged, but as a teenager, I didn't feel any compulsion to spend time with him nor did I feel that I was missing some piece in my family life. That feeling changed as I spent time in the Lawson home. I suddenly realized how deeply I craved having a father.

So I chose one. Later that year, I remember purchasing a Father's Day card for Roy and in it making some awkward statement letting him know how much the relationship meant to me. That made it formal. I was a member of the family, and Roy Lawson was my father.

I spent the next year attending Arizona State University as a physics major. My life consisted of attending classes, doing homework, and spending most of my free time in various youth and service programs at the church. I also spent a lot of time eating food out of the Lawson's refrigerator and watching rented movies on their VCR.

After a year of me dropping by unannounced, Roy asked me if I wanted a room. I think I surprised him when I said yes. Rosa, an exchange student, had already taken Lane's room so Lane was sleeping on the couch. Kim was leaving for Milligan in a month and Rosa would be leaving soon after. But before those rooms were available, I was able to claim the couch, and Lane, four years my junior, was relegated to the floor *behind* the couch. I liked that arrangement. It gave me the opportunity every Monday, Wednesday and Friday on the way to my 7:40 a.m. class at ASU, to exit the couch-bed by *stepping on Lane*. You understand, I wanted to share the joy of waking at 6:00 AM with a fifteen-year-old, and clarify that he was now my little brother. He handled it well most of the time.

For the next six months, before leaving for Bible college, I lived with the Lawson family and cemented my place as an older brother and son.

Before moving in I remember going with Roy on a number of hospital calls, several to see people with terminal conditions. I was surprised by how he handled those interactions. My instincts would have been all wrong. I would have looked at the floor, spoken in the most somber of tones, and let those people know how sorry I was for them. In contrast, Roy looked them in the eye, took them firmly by the hand and addressed their most personal issues, even their likely death. He used his characteristic teasing even in that delicate setting, and it had the remarkable effect of putting dying people at ease.

On one trip with Roy he asked me how I was enjoying the physics major I was pursuing, mentioning that he would have thought I'd have pursued more of a people-oriented line of work. I don't think he was fishing, but the conversation got me thinking. My church experience and my time within the Lawson family was compelling and powerful to me. Within a few months I made the decision to leave ASU and go to Bible college to enter the ministry, a decision sparked by my relationship with the church and the Lawsons.

Bible college and my years in ministry were wonderful experiences. I graduated from Manhattan Christian College, having attended with my two best friends, Kevin and Bruce. After graduating, I began my youth ministry as an intern at Christ's Church of the Valley, which led to a four-year term as the youth pastor at Christ's Church of Fountain Hills.

Following Fountain Hills, I spent several years getting established as a real estate agent and investor, but the offer of a position at Central Christian and the chance to work with Roy at my home church pulled me back into the ministry. I began a seven-year stint as an associate pastor before returning full-time to real estate investing.

I give you that history to make it clear that my years in the ministry were intimately related to my place in the Lawson family. Church life was an extension of my family life, which had grown around the Lawson family.

There were others like me. I had met both Jeff and Carolyn, and knew they held a similar place in the Lawson home. At some point, Roy started referring to us as his "Velcro family." The phrase captured the fundamental essence of how this evolving clan worked.

In the years that followed I enjoyed many positive moments in the Velcro family, but we also shared each other's tragedies. Shawn's and Lane's deaths, the sons respectively of Jeff and Joan and Roy and Joy, were the beginnings of our annual week together. Following Lane's death, Jeff and Joan, remembering Roy and Joy helping them through their loss of Shawn just five years before, drove us as a family around Oregon for a week as we dealt with the service and other arrangements. We learned that even in our darkest moments, maybe *especially* during our darkest moments, we liked being together. Our family vacation week was birthed in the midst of that heartache. I later lost my own brother and stepfather in a small plane crash, and, unsurprisingly, the Velcro family stepped in to carry the weight of my grieving and to handle many details of the service.

Roy and Joy and I have endured the prolonged pain of the real estate crash in 2008. We had been investing together since the late 1980s. It had all gone quite well, and we had acquired more equity than we ever expected to have. Then suddenly it was gone. Further, we found ourselves "upside down." The market crashed so hard that our debt far exceeded the value of the houses, and far exceeded anything we could reasonably expect to pay back. Our corporate bankruptcy was a tense, frightening, and depressing period.

We eventually recovered, but at the time I didn't think we would. I spent many hours crying into the phone as I reviewed our options with Roy. In spite of that pain I never for a moment thought our bond wouldn't survive that loss. Today, I wouldn't wish going through that hell on anyone, but the experience of having come out of it with my most significant relationships intact is something I wouldn't trade, even for the calm shores I was so longing for at the time. There's no shortcut to the depth of connection you feel by having been in those trenches with someone. You know you are sticking together. Just like Velcro.

Labels matter. Part of what has made this thing work is the implicit commitment that label implies. The incredibly fun times we've had together is an easy sell. But you're not a family if that's where the connection ends. Woven into the formula is a tacit understanding that we carry one another's burdens.

This Velcro family is a miracle, and I recognize how fortunate I am to be a part of it. It was instigated by a charismatic patriarch with a gift for loving people, a willingness to spend his time and treasure helping them gather together, and a talent for inspiring others to do the same. He demonstrated for us what this family's culture was to be, modeled after the values of Jesus, bringing in outsiders, recognizing our foibles, and turning our collective mishaps into badges of honor through storytelling. His wife and children not only welcomed the intrusion of aliens into their midst, but dragged in newcomers, sharing with us all some of their most intimate family moments.

For forty years I've engaged with this group. We've played together, celebrated victories, endured heartbreak, tolerated annoying differences, raised each other's kids, and shared sublime moments of reflection and disclosure. Just like a family. We are a family. A Velcro family.

10

Mike Prior

Mike Prior

WE HAD TO MAKE an exception to a fundamental rule for membership in our Velcro family ("You can't get in if you're from a functional family"). Although Mike had hung around us for years, attending the Velcro family vacations, helping me on some of the tours I led, and in many other ways occupying a special niche with us, he was not qualified to be a full-fledged member of the Velcro family. He is from a *functional* birth family. His parents, Bob and Dorothy Prior, were two of the finest church members I've ever worked with. Bob was an elder in the Mesa church when we hit town. Dorothy was in charge of the church kitchen. Both were tireless workers. No one was more respected.

In those days Bob was nearing retirement as an engineer with General Motors' Buick Division. To give you an idea of our regard for the Priors, when he did retire we made up a dual paid position on the staff for them: church host and hostess. He was pretty much in charge of the church facility; she oversaw all events using the kitchen and fellowship hall and eventually was in charge of all church weddings. They worked outrageous hours. We paid them only what Social Security allowed in those days—for *one*. But they both gave more than forty hours a week. Money wasn't their motivation, obviously. They simply loved the Lord, loved the church, and loved the work. When I tried to get them to take time off for rest and recreation, they protested, "But this work *is* our recreation."

So for years Mike couldn't officially join our Velcro family, but as I said, he's been in the middle of it since he and I worked together from the start of our Mesa ministry. He was already on the staff when I joined it. His full-time job was as a test driver for General Motors' Testing Grounds in Mesa. His position as our children's ministry director was part-time, though he always treated it like another full-time job. Before long he accepted our invitation to leave General Motors and join the church staff full time.

He held several jobs over the years, excelling in all of them: first children's minister, then church business administrator. In that role he computerized the operation (this was the early eighties), built buildings, balanced budgets, managed the office and other support staff—and so much more. In time he accepted his third assignment, becoming our executive pastor, heading the ever-growing pastoral staff.

But then we lost him. An opening appeared for "the job he was born for" (my description) as head of Financial Planning Ministries based in Orange County, California. I had to encourage him to take it, even though I felt like I was losing my right arm. He's been president of FPM for over twenty years now, during which FPM has raised over a billion dollars in expectancies for Christian charitable organizations.[1]

---

1. "Expectancies" needs a bit of an explanation. FPM writes wills and trusts for people for free if they include a bequest of any amount to at least one of its supporting entities like Central Christian Church or World Vision. Every year of Mike's presidency has seen this steady increase in what these benevolent institutions can expect from people's trusts.

I should mention one of his special roles in Mesa. In our early years the church regularly staged pageants for Christmas and Easter under the direction of Deborah May Hollenbach, our music and worship pastor. She was the first staff member we called after I became pastor. We worked together for twenty years. Early on she sized Mike up for the role he performed year after year. He was Jesus. Mike was tall, thin but not skinny, poised, bearded—and willing. He was especially effective on Palm Sundays, when as Jesus he followed the children waving palm branches into the sanctuary. He also perfected the crucifixion scenes. I may have been responsible for his retirement from the role, though, when I noted, before the congregation I'm afraid, that I had never thought of Jesus' having love handles before. I shouldn't have said it. My comments made Mike feel self-conscious. I still feel guilty. Some observations should be stifled. (I might have said that before on these pages.)

Well, Mike's now an official member of the Velcro family. We had to wait until his saintly parents died. When they did and he was orphaned (by this time he was in his fifties), we held a special ceremony at family vacation to dub him a full-fledged member of the family.

Mike's Reflections—Becoming Velcro

It's kind of funny. It draws you in. You've heard the word before but never associated it with people.

That innocent looking little strip that grabs like the Kraken and won't let go. Velcro, "to fasten, fix or join." Yes, that aptly describes this collection of people who over decades have become part of a unique assembly who, among other supportive gestures, gather round the campfire each summer, hold hands, and tell stories. Burning Man meets Hee Haw.

For years I was the outsider. Wearing the mark of PP (perfect parentage), I listened while others quietly reflected on the challenges of their often difficult, dysfunctional upbringing.

"But wait, it's not my fault. I had nothing to do with who my parents were." And that's just the point. So many struggle to overcome the hand they're dealt. I had no struggle, no excuse. I enjoyed my parents' safe harbor until time took them away.

And when that day came this group recognized that I, too, would need a safe harbor. They welcomed me with ceremony and stories, reflections and song.

Part 1: Meet Our Velcro Family

It is said you can choose your friends but you can't choose your family. When this group gathers round the reunion campfire, the great satisfaction is knowing that this is family by choice.

11

Rosa Viteri Bellettini

Rosa (right) with her daughter, Gianna

I MENTIONED ROSA ABOVE. She was one of the five teenagers living with us for a short while. Rosa's parents had sent her to live with relatives in Mesa while a student at Mountain View High School, where our kids attended. After four months Rosa asked the school counselor to help her find another host family. The counselor asked Kim if our family could take Rosa in, since Kim had earlier applied to be a foreign exchange student herself, although she wasn't able to go. Of course Kim said yes, even though she herself would be leaving for college in the fall. Rosa became ours.

She was a delight, a Latina beauty. Her coal-black hair, her brown skin, her wide, expressive eyes, easy laughter, and captivating accent charmed us all. We were glad she joined us.

One of our unforgettable memories of Rosa occurred in 1982. I was president of the North American Christian Convention (the one in which our kids' youth choir sang) in Kansas City, Missouri that year. The convention provided a commodious hotel room for the family so we could all be together. Rosa checked out the hotel's newsstand in the lobby and picked up a few magazines, probably wanting something to read during the dull speeches at the convention. Rosa had dreams of becoming an architect, so as she hurriedly made her selection she picked up one on penthouses. When she got back to our hotel room she looked more carefully at her purchases. That's when she discovered *Penthouse* wasn't about penthouses but was a pretty raunchy knockoff of *Playboy*. She blushed, we laughed, and she disposed of her purchase.

During her year in our house her mother and sister came for a visit from Ecuador. We discovered then how close her family was. The father couldn't come along; he remained in Quito, where he was the national superintendent of schools, but he was fully supportive of this opportunity for his daughter to learn more of North America. Wanting to show Rosa's family a good time, we drove to Tlaquepaque, then a fashionable mall on the edge of Sedona in Arizona's red rock country. We found a good Mexican restaurant for lunch. Several of us ordered a shrimp salad. Rosa's mother was horrified. She wouldn't let her daughter eat it. The small shrimp, she said, was considered bait in Ecuador. No self-respecting person would eat bait! A good lesson for us in cultural differences.

Another fun incident during their stay came at our dinner table. Mother, aunt, and cousin were giggling among themselves. We wondered about it until Rosa reported that they were asking her why our left hands were in our laps. Were we lame? In their culture the left forearm rests on the table.

I wish I could report that Rosa has remained a Velcro daughter. We gave her up only reluctantly. In those days the Velcro label hadn't been appropriated yet. And once again we had to admit Rosa wasn't qualified: Hers was a good family (although as time went on we discovered some practices that we questioned, as she must have also done with us). So by our regulations we couldn't "Velcro" her in. We would have found a way around this technicality, though, if she'd wanted it.[1]

We were proud of all three teenagers during Rosa's time with us. We didn't learn until much later that they didn't always find living together easy. Brought up in another country and a different family, Rosa's ways didn't always parallel our ways. Rather than complain to us, Candy and Lane and Rosa dealt with the differences themselves. They would tell this part of our story from a perspective at variance from ours, I suspect. Still, all the children have expressed a wish that we could have maintained our ties with Rosa.[2]

When she returned to her homeland, we naturally drifted apart. We did reconnect one afternoon years later in Florida. Joy and I parked there awhile in our motor home tour of America (2003–2004). By then she had married, had a daughter, and returned to the States. It was really a treat to see Rosa again and meet her daughter, Gianna. That was our last time together. We tried emailing and telephoning following the brief visit but couldn't connect. As you can tell from the teasing stories we still love to tell, we'll never forget Rosa.

1. We did subsequently visit Rosa and her family in Ecuador, where we were treated with every kindness.

2. Candy has corrected me. "It wasn't all bad with Rosa. She was a good audience for my silliness, egging me on with, 'Oh Candy,' you crack me out!'"

12

Barbara and Karrina Domke

Barbara and Karrina Domke

BARBARA DOMKE CAME INTO our lives many years before she came into our Velcro family—again, we caused the delay by moving away. One day Barb appeared at the church seeking some spiritual assistance. She was in trouble. She was pregnant. The father was a married man with no intention of taking responsibility. She was terrified of disappointing her family. (By now we were in the 1980s, but the sexual revolution of the 1960s hadn't changed *all* of society.)

That first conversation led to many, many others. I introduced her to some of the leading women in our church, who immediately adopted her. They took her with them to their annual women's retreat. They held a baby shower for her. They "showered" her, in other words, with unconditional love.

Barb carried her baby to full term, refusing both the abortion and adoption options. Instead she set her strenuous course. She would work, she would pursue more education, and she would be a good mother to Karrina. She would be faithful to her church. She accomplished all her goals.

When Joy and I left Arizona for California, the bond between us and the Domkes was stretched—but it never snapped. Barb reached out from time to time by phone and email to let us know how her life was going and how Karrina was growing—and presenting her own challenges. That sometimes rebellious daughter, by the way, is now in grad school preparing for a future in youth ministry.

Barb would tell her side of the story a little differently, undoubtedly, but she would also do what she's always done. She's never failed to express gratitude that I was there for her in those days. But my side of the story is this: No one who has come for counseling over the years has been more appreciative, more vocal about that appreciation, and more of a source of ongoing encouragement for her former counselor. It has never surprised me that she has made a good life for herself and Karrina. Her positive spirit and abiding faith have carried her far.

Karrina Domke's Story

About me: My mother was always a role model of what I could accomplish, but I did choose the wrong path and during my undergrad years really struggled to follow God and move forward. If she could get her degree while caring for me as a single mom, I had to be able to do the same without a child, but that was not always clear. After joining the wrong crowd and choosing a dangerous path, there was a while when things weren't looking good for my future. When my mother asked for advice from Roy and Joy, they told her she needs to let me fall the rest of the way. As hard as it was for my mother, they were absolutely correct. After hitting my lowest, my entire life changed, and God took over. I still had challenges but eventually graduated from my undergrad and was able to turn my life around. Now I am a certified facilitator of Mending the Soul, will be completing my master's degree in Christian leadership, and will also be starting my internship with the small group and adult ministry at my church. I am excited to see where God will take me next. It has always been amazing to have such role models like Roy and Joy in my life, even when they didn't live here.

Being a part of this Velcro family means a lot because sometimes real families can be hard. It is amazing to have a group of people willing to accept you just the way you are. There is no question as to why you belong or if you belong. You simply are a part of the family, and that is all that matters. While I still feel new to the family I have been in for a long time, seeing the love those people have for one another is inspiring. I am excited to learn more about this family.

13

Darrin and Julie Ronde

Three generations of the Darrin Ronde Family

I'VE BEEN FOLLOWING A kind of chronological order in these sketches, but it does get confused in the Mesa years. Here's a good example: Where should I put the Rondes? They do belong in these Mesa years, to be sure, but whom should I talk about first, Julie or Darrin?

I'll start with Darrin. When he first came to Central he was an alumnus of Nebraska Christian College and had already completed a couple years of graduate work at Cincinnati Christian Seminary. His plan was to spend a year in our church's internship program and then return to Cincinnati to finish his master's degree. He wanted to be a youth minister, he said, so we placed him in the youth department, but since Mike Prior had more than he could handle with the church finances and a burgeoning children's ministry, Darrin was soon asked to oversee the preschool ministry, where he impressed us all. So much so, in fact, that we offered him a full-time position—not in youth, where we didn't have an opening, but in the children's department, where we did.

Some people are just going to do well wherever you place them. That was—is—Darrin. When we signed him on we asked for his promise to give us five years. (That request, by the way, stemmed from my conviction that it's as important for a church's associate ministers to have long ministries as it is for the senior pastor. You can't build a growing, stable church with frequent turnover on the ministerial staff.) Darrin promised us five—then gave us ten. When he left for another position in Colorado, we were sorry to see him go, not only because we were losing a valuable team member but also because he was taking Velcro daughter Julie, his wife, and Velcro granddaughter Stephi and grandson Tyler with him.

Now about Julie. We got her because our daughter Kim married her brother, Royce. Kim became acquainted with Royce in December of 1984 and married him the next May. In January of 1985, Royce introduced her to his sister, Julie. Julie and her first husband David were still together, but they separated shortly after Kim and Royce were married. It was quickly apparent that Royce had done Kim a favor; thanks to him Julie and Kim became—and have remained—sisters.

When Darrin and Julie first met, Julie was the mother of as cute a two-year-old little girl as you've ever met. I still can't help wondering whether Darrin fell in love first with Julie or Stephanie. Either way, he ended up loving both.

One day Darrin stopped me in the stairway next to the choir rehearsal room. He had some serious questions to ask me about marriage. He wondered whether it would cause difficulty getting hired in the future as a pastor if he married a divorced woman. In some parts of the country and some denominations, people get really touchy about these things. Darrin says I assured him that outside the Bible belt, and especially in the West, it wouldn't be an insuperable problem. It definitely wouldn't be an issue at Central. (You have to understand—both of us knew he was talking about

Julie, whose story our church leaders knew.) I then posed a question to Darrin: What kind of man did he believe Julie should marry? He said he hoped she'd marry someone that loved her for who she was, a man that would be dedicated to raising her daughter as his own and give both of them the kind of life God desired for them. I replied[1], "And why can't you be that man?" He nodded with the assurance that it was making more and more sense to do what his heart was leading him to do. A few weeks later, they were engaged and planning a May wedding.

A highlight for me came at the conclusion of the ceremony, when the preacher—that would be me—escorted the now three-year-old Stephi up the aisle and into the foyer.

(Okay, I have to break the continuity here to tell you about another time when I was honored to escort Stephi. By this time she was a college senior and I was the soon-to-be-retired president of her college. Every spring the school hosted a formal spring banquet; that year it was on the Queen Mary, permanently docked in Long Beach. Just a few weeks before the event my phone rang. It was Stephi. "Grandpa, will you take me to the banquet?" Would I? Would a sixty-four-year-old geezer date a beautiful coed at her request? Of course I would. But why did she ask?

(Well, it turns out that several weeks earlier she had accepted the invitation of a good friend to be his companion for the evening. In the meantime, however, he had begun to get serious about another young woman and asked if Stephi would mind . . . She didn't. But she still wanted to go to the dinner dance. In desperation, she called Grandpa. And the old man, flattered, a bit flustered, jumped at the chance. I even bought my date a posy. I had a great time. I probably embarrassed her. You see, since I had already announced my retirement, they couldn't fire me. So I just became a teenager again and made a fool of myself on the dance floor. Stephi was tolerant.

(She was also looking forward to the rest of the evening when things would be looking up. I had to have her back to the dorm fairly early; another guy was waiting in line!)

Back to Darrin and Julie. They were quickly absorbed into our Velcro family, as was Stephi. Then an eagerly anticipated Tyler came along a year later. This story could have been otherwise, though. When Royce and Kim had married, he turned to his three siblings and said in effect, "Come on

---

1. I'm relying on Darrin's memory for this conversation. I've been so reluctant to play matchmaker over the years I'm having a little difficulty believing I said what Darrin says I said. But since he has such a reputation for honesty, and I have such a reputation for my poor memory, I yield to his report.

in. This family stuff is good!" His birth family was a study in dysfunction. His mother was single at this time, but she'd been married to or lived with several men. Royce and Julie were full brother and sister, but half-brothers Bill and Brett had other fathers. Their mother was a preacher's daughter, but she had spent her life rebelling against her father and the church. Her children had a lot to overcome.

(Well, I must take us on another brief detour here so you'll know what happened to Kim when her marriage to Royce dissolved. In the beginning their marriage went fairly well, but soon the fissures began appearing. Finally, after eleven years of trying, Kim became a single mom with three little boys. We were proud of Kim's strength as she faced up to and adroitly managed all her challenges. We stood by to extend help when she asked for it. But she never asked. Then, sooner than we anticipated, we learned that some of her good friends in the church had decided Kim needed to get to know Ed Thompson, a single father who was volunteering in the youth department and who, these well-intentioned busybodies agreed, would be the perfect match for Kim. They were right.

(Our family has watched in amazement as Kim and Ed have led their blended family—Kim's Kyle, Nick and Luke, and Ed's Breanne and Nicholas[2]—through so many trials and crises. And through them all, Kim's and Julie's mutual adoption has held firm. When Julie's brother Royce left the family, he did his best to take his brothers and sister out with him. He had become convinced that all the Lawsons were no good. But Julie wouldn't leave us. Out of that tragic situation has come an unbreakable bond.)

OK, I haven't forgotten that this this section is supposed to be about Darrin and Julie. We have marveled that Julie, given her background, took so well to her new role as a pastor's wife. We knew all along that Darrin had the "stuff" to be an outstanding minister; his work in Mesa and Colorado Springs has proved us right. But to see Julie jump in and help him in every way she could has been really rewarding. Given her mother's rebellion against her parents and the church and the frequent neglect of her four children, Julie had every excuse for turning against both church and marriage. But she didn't. Instead, she has worked to overcome her past and has given herself fully to the present. Along the way she developed her own gifts. (She's an accomplished accountant, an effective women's minister, and

---

2. Yes, you read that right. Both parents contributed a Nicholas. And the two Nicholases are almost exactly the same age. So, to minimize confusion, we have Nicholas—and Nick.

an advocate for world missions who has led numerous groups to visit mission fields around the globe.) And she and Darrin have guided Stephi and Tyler to maturity and effective parenthood.

I've enjoyed talking shop with Darrin on our all-family vacations. We plan on at least one coffee date during the week. The whole family loves Darrin, especially his quick wit. When he presided over the mock wedding in which he remarried Joy and me as part of our fiftieth anniversary celebration, he turned what should have been a solemn occasion into a roast. It was delicious.

We never met Darrin's father, but we understand he was not an easy man to live with. We did get to know his mother, though. She lived into her nineties. What a gracious, witty, utterly charming, indomitable woman. She even regularly bowled until shortly before she died. Getting acquainted with her gave us the explanation we sought. No wonder Darrin turned out so well. Betty was his mother! He and the rest of us treasure the memories of Betty getting to experience his "other" crazy family at our all-family vacation in Branson in 2017. She joined the rest of us on a boat ride on Table Rock Lake at the invitation of Ted Cunningham, a well-known local pastor, comedian, and author. Darrin says she talked of that outing often until she died.

Darrin's take on the Velcro Family story is actually incorporated in what I wrote about him above. I sent him my rough draft and he corrected it. (It was less than perfect.) Then Julie read what Darrin had sent in and gave her stamp of approval. So we turn now to the Ronde kids' story, first my perspective, then from Stephi and her husband Tom. Tyler trusts his sister and brother-in-law to tell the story right.

Tom and Stephi Arbaugh

Tom and Stephanie with Eden, Elias, and Estin in 2019

The little girl I walked up the church aisle and later dated at the university's dinner dance gave me yet another thrill just a few years later. "Grandpa, will you marry me?" Of course I would. The groom would be Tom Arbaugh, whom Stephi had met while they were both on the staff of a Christian youth camp. We took him in because we believed in Stephi, but for a while we weren't so sure about this guy. He was a new Christian. That was good. But he had been a teenage rebel. That could have been problematic. He had tattoos!

One day I screwed up enough courage to ask, "Stephi, you've always been a good girl. What did you see . . . ?"

She cut me off with a grin. "Good girls like bad boys." Turns out, though, that Tom may once have been a bad boy but he's anything but a bad man. After they both finished their further studies in Chico, California, Tom packed up his new family and they headed to Tennessee—to go for a Master of Divinity degree at Emmanuel Christian Seminary, where I would join him later when I picked up my third career, this one as a seminary professor.

A moment I've never forgotten: Chaplain Heather Holland taught an orientation class for new students once a week during fall semester. I wasn't yet on the seminary faculty but was a visiting professor that semester at Milligan College across the highway. She asked me to come for a lunch session in which she would interview me on my ministerial experience. When the floor was open for student questions, Tom was the first one to speak. "Tell them about the Velcro family," he said. He hadn't been "ours" very long, but he already saw it as something special. I was proud to brag about our family, and already proud to speak of Tom as a member.

In East Tennessee Tom picked up two master's degrees, his Master of Divinity from Emmanuel and a master's in counseling from Milligan College. He also worked as both chaplain and counselor, helping to support their three children. Stephi took on the task of primary breadwinner with Mary Kay while he was in school. She's done pretty well. She drives a pink Cadillac.

The best part of their living in Johnson City, though, was what this meant for the great-grandparents. When we had lived in Mesa and so did Kim and Ed and their kids, we had the joy of having grandchildren around: Kyle, Nick and Luke and Nicholas and Bre. And until the Rondes moved away, Stephi and Tyler. And Velcro grandkids—Rich and Patti's kids, Casey and Jayne's, and toward the end of our time in Mesa, Jeff and Joan's daughter Kim and her first husband Bob (and daughter Madi and son Cade—Joel was born later in Bakersfield).

In Johnson City we once again had grandkids and *great*-grandkids nearby. What a favor Tom and Stephi did us. For holidays, for other special occasions, and just because we wanted to, we'd get together. One of my favorite memories from East Tennessee comes from the last half-year we were there. As I was closing out my teaching career at Emmanuel Christian Seminary, I was also the *ad interim* minister of First Christian Church. The best moments of the Sunday morning services came after the third one when, as most of the people were filing out of the auditorium, I heard the laughter and footsteps of three little children who were gunning for Grandpa. They hit with such force they nearly toppled me over. And at least one time it was not "nearly"!

Other unforgettable moments from those final months in Tennessee, both Arbaugh related: One Sunday morning Tom baptized his firstborn, Eden. Grandpa had a little trouble with moisture in his eyes. And on another Sunday, I had the privilege of conducting an ordination service for Tom and two other young men from the church. I was doing this for Stephi's "bad boy," remember. Ask me if I was proud.

It's a strange thing, this business of grandparenting. I don't know whether our experience has been unique, but I doubt it has. It seems to be more fun with each new generation. I don't think we've ever adequately thanked Tom and Stephi for making it so. We were pretty old in our Emmanuel years—I took up this new career when I was 73. They were gentle with us, not expecting us to babysit (I, at least, would have been terrified) or take on other normal grandparenting chores. They knew our limitations and respected them. On the other hand, they granted us great grandparents all the privileges we could have asked for.

One more story. When Stephi was pregnant with Estin, their third child, Tom was awarded a free trip to the Holy Land, a real honor. We all encouraged him to accept, even though it would mean leaving Stephi for a couple weeks with two little children (Eden and Elias) and one brand new baby. Aunt Kim flew in from Seattle to help out. She had been Mommy Kim to Stephi when she was little and came to pick up her "parental" duties once again. She didn't know how much she would be needed. Estin scared us all. He wasn't able to nurse properly; he was losing weight. He became listless. None of us knew what to do.

When Tom returned he saw the difference in Estin's appearance that had eluded us who were with him every day; Tom immediately arranged for Estin to be hospitalized. The baby remained in the hospital for a week. Great Grandpa and Great Grandma remained close by. Stephi has said she didn't know what she'd have done during that week "without our family there."

Here was but one of many, many times when the strength of a Velcro family was on full display. The great grandparents were on hand. Stephi's Mommy Kim was there until Tom got home and took charge. During the whole trauma the family came through. You understand why I'm telling this story? Estin's great grandparents and Great Aunt Kim aren't related by blood. Just by love. That's what this Velcro business is all about.

They Speak for Themselves—Stephi

It all started when a single mom[3] found Central. I spent lots of time at Mommy Kim's house while my mom worked to support us. That's when we found them. Our family. My mom and I both come from fractured roots. When I was three my mom married Darrin, the children's pastor at Central. Grandpa conducted the ceremony while Grandma and Kim helped everything and everyone look beautiful. As a child I remember Christmas Eves at Grandma's, visiting the fairy-tale Payson house, Grandma's amazing meals

3. Julie Drain, who before long became Julie Ronde.

and crafts and Grandpa's ability to make you feel like you were the only one in the room. I knew I was important and loved.

We have followed each other around the country in the decades that followed. I count this as one of my dearest blessings. We lived in L.A. together while I was in undergrad at Hope and just six years later they followed us to Tennessee. Home had followed us to the far reaches of the Appalachian Mountains. Thanksgivings and Christmas were again at Grandma's. The rich aromas coming from the kitchen of her beautiful house are the same wherever you find them. Listening to Grandpa preach at First Christian sweeps me away to my childhood and Central. Now my children sit and listen and know they are loved.

This family is the greatest gift. When family had abandoned me, creating rifts and wounds, this family stepped in to heal. You couldn't shake them if you tried. Grandma has listened, taught me so many things, sat huddled with me under blankets to watch the boys do more waving than playing T-Ball. Grandpa has taught me what Jesus looks like, how to walk in joy and love above all else, and counseled me through many tough seasons One of my favorite things is conversations with Grandma and Grandpa. I am not a sentimental person but Grandma's quilt covers me when I sleep and her oven pancakes complete Christmas. Grandpa's writing desk sits in our house and inspires the writer in me and my daughter.

They Speak for Themselves—Tom

I grew up going to church. While I do have some fond memories and it wouldn't be fair to characterize it as all bad, our particular community was not a safe place to explore and ask questions. It was mostly a breeding ground for shame and exclusive tribalism. For a young man with some particularly painful adverse childhood experiences, this environment was destined to become a catalyst for a launch into a rebellious adolescence. As many of these tales go, I eventually crashed at the proverbial rock bottom and crawled back to faith as a broken prodigal. Even so, church and I were like oil and water for many years.

Six months into my faith journey, I felt a call to return home to a Christian summer camp. I was still a bit of a novice at the whole religious thing. You might even say "a bit rough around the edges." I had the sense to quit smoking since I'd be around kids, but others pointed out that my testimony might offend if I kept cursing, and for the sake of the parents I might want to cover the tattoos or remove some piercings. There was no hiding that I was attending a state school; I stuck out quite a bit from my peers who had all been recruited from various Bible schools. And one of them stuck out to me . . .

When I first met Stephanie I thought it would never work. At best I figured it would be a Romeo and Juliet story, where our two worlds would just be too far apart. These fears were only magnified when I learned she came from a family of pastors (yikes!). But I was smitten and just as stubborn as I had always been, so I pursued. Not sure if it was my Jeep or that Pastor Kids like to feel a little edgy too, but something worked. Lucky for us, our colleges were 500 miles from one another. Thus, our entire courtship was over the phone. We had nothing to do but talk. It was in one of these conversations that Stephanie first challenged my relationship with God.

At this point in my journey, I was still pretty wary of church. I would say things like, "God and I are good. It's God's people I'm still not sure about." To which Stephanie would frankly retort, "You think that you and God can be good while you talk about his Bride that way?" (Who says women can't preach?!) It was also around this time that I first heard about "the Velcros." Stephanie tried to tell me how they all fit together, but one thing I remember most is her saying, "Don't worry, you'll fit right in. You'll love them. And they'll love you." I wasn't so sure, knowing that the patriarch was a pastor, but I was intrigued.

All my doubts evaporated when I started meeting these people and hearing their stories. For one thing, most of them had woven plenty of their own sordid tales. I realized quickly that I wasn't going to be the riffraff everyone had to watch out the corner of their eyes in this group! They were absolutely broken. And undeniably beautiful. I am not exaggerating when I say that the first "church" I trusted was this one. The Velcros became my first vision of what the Kingdom of God is. It is a community where questions and learning are encouraged, failure and grace are expected, and hope and love always prevail.

Tyler and Corrine Ronde

Tyler and Corrinne with Rowan and Aedan

There was great rejoicing when Tyler Ronde was born. He's Julie's only son, Darrin's only biological child. By now, though, you have learned that "by blood" doesn't mean any more than "by love" in this family. Some of our Velcros are related by blood; all are related by love. So Joy and I can't claim either Stephi or Tyler as our biological grandchildren. But they certainly are our love grandchildren.

Tyler and Stephi could have provided a case study for the pop psychology books on birth order that were best sellers a few decades ago. Stephi was the stereotypical first child who pleases her parents to get attention. Tyler, finding that "pleasing" slot already filled by his big sister, came into the world determined to get their attention by *not* always conforming. He was a challenge every step of the way to adulthood. Yet he was also intelligent, witty, and proud to be a Ronde. And as a teenager, so far as this doting grandfather could tell, he didn't "smoke or chew or go with the girls who do." (I learned that line from my old preacher, who used it to describe *smug* Christians—which Tyler definitely wasn't.) I don't think he ever took up drinking or drugs or any of the other popular vices of American youth. He worried his preacher father a bit, I suspect, by his dallying about becoming a Christian—but that day came in his twenties when Tyler was good and ready!

As I write this section I have been reflecting on the man Tyler has become. Unfortunately, as with so many others of our grandchildren, Joy and I didn't live in the same town and didn't have many opportunities to hang around during the growing-up years. We still don't live near each other, but we've had some important times together, like the 2019 family vacation in Tillamook, the first for Tyler in several years and the first opportunity for him to show off *his* family to the rest of us.

Like his father, Tyler fell in love with a beautiful single mother. In this case he gained not a daughter but a son, Aeden. The rest of us fell in love with them also. I hope Tyler and Corrine could feel how proud I was to preside at their outdoor wedding near Colorado Springs, the third time I got to marry a member of the Ronde family.

For quite some time we thought Tyler would make a career of photography—but with the advent of smartphone cameras everybody's a photographer now, so that's not the most promising career field. Instead, Tyler—a natural teacher—has been preparing for a teaching career. Corrine's a social worker. Neither career will make the younger Rondes rich. In money, that is. But both offer their own real rewards.

Tyler and Corrine are now the parents of two delightful little boys. Aeden was joined by Rowan in 2017.

14

Jayne and Casey Reynolds

Two World Converge

Casey and Jayne with Emily, Brittany and Naomi

I LOVE TELLING THEIR story. It began long ago and far away, in England's Midlands. In the early 1980s my friend Bob Wetzel invited me to join the governing board of Springdale College, a ministry-preparation school he was establishing in cooperation with leaders of the British Churches of Christ. It was one of nine cooperating Selly Oak colleges affiliated with the University of Birmingham. For nineteen out of the next twenty years, thanks to Principal Wetzel, I flew to England for the annual college board meeting, one of my most enjoyable assignments.

I didn't know anything about our British churches and understood even less about how to do college in the UK. But I had long since learned to trust Dr. Wetzel. When I arrived at Milligan College in 1965, Bob had already been on the faculty for four years. He had his Ph.D. in philosophy; I held a brand-new master's degree in English. I was as green as any aspiring college teacher could be. Bob quickly sized up my academic innocence and took me under his wing. I owed—and owe—him much, so when he asked for my help in getting his new college off the ground I couldn't hesitate.

As I recall I met the senior Sewell family the first year the board convened. Bob housed us American trustees in the homes of students and other friends of the college. Jayne's father had joined the student body as soon as there was a college to join, feeling called to study for the ministry. When Bob appealed for volunteer hosts for the visiting trustees, Chris and his wife Pat stepped up. They drew my name. Pat was almost beside herself with nervousness. Apart from extended family, she and Chris had never hosted overnight guests—let alone an alien from America. And you know, I can be pretty scary!

Not to worry. They showed me every courtesy, and I immediately fell in love with five-year-old Jayne and her younger brother Mark. It was not only love at first sight, but it was a love built to last.

Several years later, thanks again to Springdale's principal, Chris brought his family to America while he pursued the year's ministerial internship required by his Springdale degree program. He had a choice of two options, one in Florida and the other, which he wisely chose, in Arizona. This brought us together again. Jayne and Mark were now a few years older, of course.

What's interesting in light of subsequent events is that Casey and Jayne did not meet that year. At the time Casey was a teenager. His family fully qualified him for membership in the Lawson Velcro family. Newly divorced, his mother, Darla, was struggling to raise her three children on her own; she and the children did not attend Central when the Sewells were there.

One more fast forward. By now Jayne is a young woman. On her own she makes her second trip to Arizona, this time to reconnect with her best friend, Bonnie. When she returned to Central Christian this time, Casey was there. They met, they connected, they made promises, and began planning a future together.

This is where Joy and I step back into the story. We were in Birmingham where I taught for a few weeks at Springdale College during my sabbatical leave from Central Christian. It just so happened—or was it providence?—that we were "in town," so I was available to marry Casey and Jayne. It was one of my most memorable weddings. The service, appropriately enough, was held in a church. I conducted the service and then, to meet the laws governing English matrimony, the local pastor intoned the proper words to make everything legal. Then we all repaired to an historic abbey for the reception, a picturesque setting that the royal family could boast of, replete with servants bedecked in medieval costumes, entertainers strutting their stuff, and tables groaning with good food and drink.

Then came the maddening negotiations through the labyrinth of America's immigration laws. Casey returned to the States shortly after the wedding, but it was multiplied weeks before Jayne could finally obtain permission to join her husband in Arizona. There they happily settled and began their family.

Quite soon. This story has to be told. When I met with the soon-to-be-newlyweds for their premarital counseling, we covered the usual requisite topics, including family planning. When I introduced that subject Jayne quickly assured me nothing more needed to be said. "We've decided we'll just accept however God blesses us." Fair enough.

So only a few weeks after they were reunited in the States, Jayne became pregnant. Nine months later Naomi was born. In no time at all Jayne was pregnant again. Nine months later Brittany was born. And her twin sister Emily (I'm not sure who came first). Now Casey and Jayne were parents of three babies thirteen months and under. The next time I saw Jayne I reminded her of their decision to be grateful for however God blessed them. "We've taken care of that," she snapped. There have been no more such blessings.

But, you ask, what does their story have to do with our Velcro family?

Just this: Over the course of time, with no explicit words having been spoken, Joy and I just assumed the role of Jayne's American parents. We were a kind of a bridge for her over the ocean separating the US from the UK. We knew each other in England before we knew each other in America. We couldn't fulfill all the parental duties, but we didn't have to. For every major event Chris and Pat, Jayne's parents, were "there" for her and Casey. And Casey's mom was also nearby. They weren't bereft of parents. Still, they let us play the part, also.

"But what about the rule that you can't get into the Lawson family if you're from a functioning one?" It's obvious the Sewells are a tight-knit, loving, functional family, but this is where Casey plays his important role. His birth family has had enough troubles to cover both him and Jayne. His father was in jail after committing a serious crime. His incarceration left a couple of pretty badly scarred children; somehow Casey escaped the worst of the consequences. Joy and I often marvel at his stability, sense of responsibility, and faithfulness to Jayne and the girls. They both exhibit excellent parenting skills; their daughters are a joy to be around.

Jayne has struggled for years with health challenges; those struggles led her to study and then become a consultant in nutrition. She's become Joy's advisor and, of course, has regularly—even if her counsel has not always been appreciated—been counselor to her own daughters. (I haven't asked them how faithfully they take her advice!)

Casey began his work for the United States Post Office as a young man. He's still there. I admire him. His devotion to his family and determination not to repeat the mistakes of his father have kept him on the job. I think what has helped him, in addition to his faith and his various ministries in the church, is his wicked (the only wicked thing about him) sense of humor. It is not good for him and Brian to get together. They goad each other on!

Another word about Casey. He recently was appointed to the top leadership council of Central Christian Church's Mesa campus. The qualities we in the family see have been observed and appreciated by his peers in the church.

About those three little babies. They're young women now. When the Reynolds, all five of them, visited us in Prescott, Arizona last year, we got to see once again how well they are maturing. Naomi, the firstborn, has taken the most pride in her individuality. She will be who she will be. Taking after her father, she has decided not to go to college. Instead she does salt-of-the-earth work with developmentally disabled adults.

Brittany and Emily are in college—but before long they won't be. They are well on the way to completing their degree programs, Emily in psychology and Brittany in graphic design. I want to live a long time, because I want to be around when they these three are fully on their own. They have a lot to offer.

Jayne and Casey Reynolds

And Now from Jayne: the British Point of View

To be honest, I can't say I remember my first meeting with the Lawsons. I was, after all, only about five years old. However, I have heard one or two tales about just how nervous my mother was about hosting an international church leader when she had barely come to faith herself.

And the rumors are true, I did grow up in an idyllic situation with a close-knit family. Constantly in and out of each other's homes, we were surrounded with the love and affection of a matriarchal great grandmother, doting grandmother, aunts, uncles, and cousins galore. On my mother's side, my grandparents lived in and worked at Croft Castle, which brought life to the fairy tales and ghost stories that inhabited my young and impressionable mind.

When my father accepted a role as an intern at Central Christian Church in August of 1985, it catapulted our family into a brand new adventure. Rumor has it that my mum had prayed and "told" God that she would go anywhere for Him but the desert. I think God chuckled as He made it so.

It began a year that was unlike anything we had ever experienced. It was the first time we had been so far outside the tight-knit bonds of our little family, in a place that was the total opposite of England's green and pleasant lands. Our year abroad opened our eyes and minds to the culture of a different people group and their societal customs and traditions. (Who knew that stringing bits of popped corn made a great Christmas decoration, that you could purchase a book that listed all of the poisonous animals of the Sonoran Desert, or that it was apparently OK for your neighbors to hold up your would-be tire thief at gunpoint?)

Looking back, it's crystal clear to me that our year in Arizona introduced me to the concept of Velcro family, although at the time I had no catchy name by which to define it. We hadn't even been stateside for a week before loving church members stepped in as surrogate family. They helped to fill the void created in our hearts by 6,000 miles, expensive phone bills, and the ancient communication system whose appropriate epithet is "snail mail."

My father is fond of repeating the line that I "hijacked his adventure." I don't know for sure when it started, but I think I got bitten by something akin to the travel bug when I was ten. Sentimental memories of blue skies and backyard pools beckoned on dreary English days, and so, when I was seventeen and eighteen, I came back to visit my best friend, Bonnie. On my second trip I met a rather handsome young man who did a terrible impersonation of an English accent. I was hooked. Seven or so years later, we were well and truly committed, for better or for worse, and up to our eyeballs in kids. And I was learning what it meant to belong to two cultures but at the same time, neither one. I was homesick and missing family.

Don't get me wrong, I still belonged to my wonderful family back in the UK, they were just 6,000 miles away. And I was married into a new little family in the US that brought with it all kinds of challenges that we'd rather call opportunities. His grandparents were foundational members of Central Christian Church, his dad had been one of the church musicians, and his mom was focused on being home to raise Casey and his two siblings until their world was shattered by egregious violations that tore any semblance of "normal" to shreds. At age twelve, Casey's dad left for the last time, and by the time Casey was nineteen, his dad was facing twelve years in prison.

My mother-in-law did everything she could to hold their family unit together and keep a roof over their heads. She was a single working mom who continued to provide for the next six years and beyond. Addiction crept into the lives of Casey's sister and brother, and his sister became a single mother to three children, two of whom found themselves being raised by their paternal families, one who ended up living with us for three years.

In 1994, about a year before our wedding, Casey's mom moved to Wisconsin where she would spend the next four years rediscovering herself and seeking a well-deserved fresh start.

So, as newlyweds, we found ourselves quite devoid of family, either because of the distance or because of the dysfunction.

Neither Casey nor I can recall exactly when we first became part of a small group Bible study with Kim (Lawson) Thompson and Velcro family member, Patti Parker-Phillips, but it was probably around the year 2000. Knowing that we were somewhat bereft of places to hang on the holidays, they invited us to one or two Lawson family get-togethers, and it wasn't long before we were persuaded to attend our first Lawson-Terrill family vacation.

Our twins turned three on that trip. We were in Colorado and far from home, but surrounded by friends who stepped up as familial pinch-hitters and knocked it out of the park. There was a walk by the lake with Aunt Candy for the twins (which may have caused me several moments of panic when they went "missing" because I didn't know where they were), rides on Aunt Julie's horse, and hours of play with new "cousins." When it came time to celebrate their birthdays, we were touched by the party that was thrown for them complete with cake and gifts. And just like that, we were hooked.

It's hard to believe eighteen years have passed since that first vacation. Those years have been filled with many a Velcro gathering, and to the best of our memory, we have attended six family vacations. The ebb and flow of life has not always permitted us to be there, but we know we were sorely missed.

Quite frankly we're not the same people we were back then. In the beginning it was really hard to understand just how treasured and wanted we were and how seriously the Lawsons took the art of loving all the waifs and strays that wandered through their door, including us. But like any kid that joins a family, we've had eighteen years to grow up into it. The longevity of our relationship with the Lawson-Terrill clan has solidified our familial ties, it has strengthened our understanding of kinship, and taken us to a level of comfort that we never thought possible. It has brought us to a place of sincere gratitude for the investment in our lives, and delight at the love and laughter we get to share.

We have been encouraged in our parenting, challenged to step up in similar ways to meet the needs of others lacking family, and schooled in the art of not taking things too seriously. We are now a long-standing part of the camp-fire stories, we add to the number that were married by "Dear Old Dad," and are now advanced enough in years to chew the cud with other "oldies" who have grown-up kids.

Velcro is an apt description for this diverse group of people that we are privileged to call family. As they have journeyed through life, they have "hooked" the dysfunctional, the broken, and the emotionally crippled, and given us a place to call home. We kind of like it. We think we'll stick around.

A Few Words from a Couple of the Reynolds Offspring

Emily

Every time I sit down and talk about our not-so-little Velcro family, I have to explain what that actually means. I'm sure we all do! But each time I explain what it means to be a family that sticks together, I'm reminded of the genuine community our little family brings. It's a group of people, rapidly growing each year, brought together and bonded through seasons of celebration and mourning alike. It's a group of people who are unashamedly authentic and real with each other. It's a group of people from all backgrounds and walks of life who have chosen to do life together in whatever that entails. Every year I look forward to unwinding and filling myself back up with the love and community that is found in our family, and I am so incredibly thankful I've been adopted into our ragtag bunch of misfits.

Brittany

Throughout my lifetime, I have been impacted by the support and relationships the Velcro family has with one another. We always know, whatever our season, that these people are willing to be present and to fill it with joy. I can think of countless times we've laughed until we cried, made fun of Brian, or gathered wisdom from those who have come before us. This family has met us where we are and cared for each other. I've loved every second of being included in this group of mischief makers!

15

Patti and Richard Phillips

Rich and Patti with their combined families except for Patti's son, JD

PATTI AND HER YOUNG son, JD, became Velcros before I was aware of it. She was already connected with Brian and Kim by the time I got acquainted with her. Brian was the twenties' pastor at Central Christian. Patti was a single mother struggling to make ends meet and to make a home for JD, five. Her deadbeat (this is an official term, by the way) husband was in the military. The marriage was virtually over. He lived abroad but was unwilling either to support his family or divorce his wife. Patti sought counsel from her pastor, Brian; he couldn't solve her marital issues but he could and did befriend her and help her find friends in the church. She became a willing volunteer for his ministry team.

Along came a Super Bowl game in January 1997. Brian told Patti he wanted to introduce her to a very close friend of his who was going through a rough time. She was recently separated and headed toward divorce. He was certain Patti could help her navigate these waters and they could be a blessing to each other. That person was our daughter Kimberly. It was the beginning of a friendship—a true sisterhood—that has lasted over twenty years. Kim's three boys and Patti's son also became quick friends as they all started "doing life together."

A happy memory of Patti comes from our retirement party at Central Christian in 1999. The sanctuary was packed to its 2,000-seat capacity at 4:00 Sunday afternoon, April 18. New lead pastor, Cal Jernigan, was presiding. He asked me to stand and help him introduce our family to the congregation. We were seated together in the front rows. Patti was beside Kim and Ed. When it was her turn to be introduced, I explained that she was our scullery maid. Patti wasn't certain whether I had complimented or insulted her.

It was a compliment, but like too many of mine, probably, it seemed a little backhanded. Here's why that word popped into my mind. For centuries, European families that could afford household help employed a scullery maid, the (usually) young woman who helped with the cooking, did the mopping and dusting and whatever else was needed. She was not the center of attention but worked quietly in the background. Without her, however, the household couldn't function.

That's Patti: never calling attention to herself, always ready to help. It was Patti, for example, who thought of and designed the T-shirts for all of us on Grandpa's seventieth birthday cruise. (Forty-two of them said, "I'm Grandpa's Favorite"; mine said, "I'm Grandpa.") She did this in spite of her personal drama—she would step off the ship and into the hospital for breast cancer surgery. Typically, she didn't ask for sympathy but instead hosted a party in Mazatlan which she labeled, "Good-bye to the Girls."

That's Patti. She certainly qualifies for membership in this family. Her birth family had its own stresses; that's where she gained the strength to support others in their traumas. Her first marriage was failing. JD, a rambunctious boy in need of a father's touch, was a challenge. In addition, she sometimes took on caring for her young nephew, the son of her brother who ended up in prison. Additionally, she tended to the needs of her aging mother, since the rest of her family lived on the east coast.

When Kim invited Patti and JD to join our family, Brian seconded the motion. And before I knew it, they were in. But at the retirement party, Cal caught me unprepared: I could label sons and daughters and sisters and grandkids—but Patti, who at that moment was just becoming solidly one of us, had no title yet. Hence "scullery maid." I can defend that impulsive description. After these decades together, she's still on the lookout for ways to serve.

I can't leave out Richard. In time Patti was able to untangle herself from the grasp of her nonsupportive, absentee husband. It was a relief. We watched her blossom. We weren't the only ones to notice. Once again Grandpa got to perform a marriage ceremony. Richard, a computer geek—and a man with a servant's heart as big as Patti's—who had had his own disappointments in marriage, brought daughters Chelsea and Ashley to join Patti and JD into their blended family. It hasn't always been easy, but they've made it work.

I asked Patti to help me sort out the Parker-Phillips household. Here's her response:

> Ashley (Richard's daughter) is an astounding woman who has always had a passion for children and recently started as the director of a brand-new children's day care facility in Gilbert. She also has a blog and shares some great insight on faith and parenting with others. Ashley is married to Sterling, an awe-inspiring father with a passion for coaching his kids and others in sports and, more importantly, in becoming responsible young people. JD (Patti's son) has grown into a magnificent, responsible, fiercely independent and adventuresome young man with a heart like his mother. He will help and give to others sacrificially out of their need and not always his familiarity with them. Chelsey [Richard's other daughter] is a spectacular single mom to Reyna and Maddox. She has a smile that lights up a room and a joy-filled spirit in spite of life's difficulties. The girls and their families are both in Arizona, which gives Richard and Patti the opportunity to be around the grandkids often and enjoy their sports and school activities as well as sleepovers. JD has recently moved to California for a five-year time frame, much to his mom's dislike. Patti has also recently added another 'kid' to her brood. A lifelong friend of hers passed away recently, and Patti now includes her niece, Riley Marcellus, as one of hers.

Patti's son, JD, and her new Velcro daughter, Riley Marcellus

I quoted Patti at length here, because it sounds so like her. She's generous even with her adjectives!

It's a wonder Richard will even come to our annual all-family vacation weeks. He must steel himself for what he knows is coming. We all have computers, which means we all have computer problems. And we all also know the one guy among us who can fix them. So Richard spends too much of his vacation playing doctor to our sick machines—or should I say playing teacher, trying to minimize each machine's operator's ignorance. Either way, the man is busy. If Patti's our scullery maid, Richard's our in-house computer handyman. In truth, though, they are Grandpa Roy's and Grandma's Joy's Velcro son and daughter. And we're grateful they're in the family.[1]

Patti and Darrin responded to my request for their input in the same way: They read what I had drafted, corrected and enlarged it, and sent it back. That means if they aren't satisfied with the published result, it's at least partially their fault. They had a chance to submit their version whole. I think

---

1. Joy traces the idea for this book to that evening around the campfire when she heard Patti's story of "How I got into the Velcro family and why I stayed." Joy thought to herself, "I'd like to hear that story again."

this also means they have total trust in my storytelling, since I have a record of never exaggerating, stretching, or missing the truth.

16

The Porous Borders

THE BOUNDARIES AROUND OUR Velcro family have holes in them. Or another way of saying the same thing: The door is always open. Sometimes we are surprised, like the time at Patti's wedding when her matron of honor told me, "I'm so glad I'm one of your Velcro kids." I didn't know she was. And she never really came all the way in, but her daughter Riley joined us for a couple of vacations and, when her mother died recently, Patti, who has always been like her second mother, stepped forward and walked her through the darkness. How did I know that? Because when Tom and Stephi invited us all to a mini-Velcro family reunion in Arizona (during the church's sixtieth anniversary celebration), Patti invited Riley, now a college freshman, to join us. She came and brought a friend with her. This was just two days after Riley's mother died. We were so glad to see her. We hope we can hang on to her forever.

Then there was the time that Mike Prior was making one of his FPM presentations to a church in New Hampshire. *Adam Tomlinson* introduced himself to Mike and explained, "I'm one of Roy's Velcro sons." When Mike repeated the incident to me, I was a little surprised. Adam feels like a Velcro son, to be sure, but I hadn't formally included him because both he and his wife Lauren are from well-functioning families. (I should explain that Adam was my PA [professor's assistant] at Emmanuel. During that year together we became good friends. Later Joy and I visited the Tomlinsons and their son Nathanael in New England. If they were closer I'd invite them to every one of our vacations. And now we'd include both sons, Nathanael *and* Caleb.)

And just before I started this book I received an email from *Steven Ostrega*. He'd read our lawsonsontheloose.net blog post about the Arizona Velcro reunion at the Arbaugh's last December. He wrote to remind me that he, too, is one of us. He speaks the truth. Our friendship began in Mesa when he was a teenager in the church. From then on, through his and our various moves, his marriage and subsequent divorce, his trials as a single father of three children, his military service, his pursuit of various preaching ministries (he's a proud Pentecostal minister), we've remained good friends. Given his parents' trials and marriages and remarriages, and then his own domestic struggles, Steve definitely has earned his way into our collection!

Just a few days ago I had a text message from *Kaitlyn Harville,* saying she's missing her "Grandpa." I'm not really her grandfather, although I sign off on my emails to her with DOG (Dear Old Grandpa). And—you won't be surprised, since by now you've learned how the Velcro Family grows—if she were closer she'd be vacationing with us. She doesn't quite qualify, though, since she's also from a close-knit, supportive family.

Kaitlyn and I met during fall semester 2010, when she was a Milligan College freshman and I was her freshman humanities professor. I was there just for a semester, substituting for a regular professor on sabbatical leave. I've teased her since about how hard she made me work. I kept the freshmen alert in class and up-to-date in their reading by foisting fairly frequent pop quizzes on them. I was almost never able to give Kaitlyn less than a grade of 100 percent. She always corrects me when I tell this story. She insists she *never* earned less than 100 percent. Surely she's wrong!

We next saw one another when I returned to East Tennessee to join the faculty of Emmanuel Christian Seminary in 2012—and she was once again my student. Earning As, of course. Then she worked as my PA. And when I was interim minister at First Christian Church during my last year with Emmanuel, I recommended her for a staff position. She was still with the church when we left East Tennessee to go on the loose.

We drew closer than the usual professor-student relationship for another reason. Kaitlyn began experiencing some severe health problems, including a bout with thyroid cancer. She and Joy commiserated on that subject, since both have had thyroid surgery. Although she is much better, she is not free of health complications to this day. Neither is she free of her old professor and his wife.

Part 1: Meet Our Velcro Family

Brenda Painchaud won Joy's heart many years ago. When Joy's mother was in the early stages of her dementia, Brenda, a practical nurse, became her caregiver. Her caring went well beyond the expectations of her profession. She treated Mrs. Whitney with the love she would give her own mother. From then on, she has been like another Velcro daughter. She and her husband, Tony, have not had easy lives, coming from their own dysfunctional birth families and then struggling through their unsuccessful first marriages before marrying each other and blending their families. Their marriage has worked, but it has been bedeviled by ill health, both his and hers, forcing them to take early retirement and to practice careful financial management. They haven't been able to participate in the annual all-family vacation with regularity, but they stay in touch, primarily through long telephone conversations between Brenda and Joy. They know the border is porous and they're always welcome to be with us.

Brenda Painchaud's Tribute to Joy

Brenda and Tony 1990s

The Velcro kids who wouldn't go away. That's Tony and me. With Velcro firmly applied, we stuck like glue to Roy and Joy 23 years ago and have stayed connected to them like Siamese twins, inseparable!

Tony and I had just got married and started attending Liberty Christian Church. After a short while, one of the honored elderly couples stood out. Being in the nursing field, I saw that Don was in need of help with caring for Elma, who was struggling with Alzheimer's. Don would ask us over for supper, and I saw it was getting more difficult to be a husband and caregiver to his cherished wife. So we decided that I would be her caregiver and he could go back to being her honored husband. Time went on until Elma required 24/7 specialized care.

Through the stages of her disease I met Joy and Roy. What a blessing this would be for years to come. I didn't grow up with a mother figure in my life and Joy became my Velcro mom. I love her so much! So from deep within my heart, I write this.

The Lord has given some of us a special mom to love. He chooses those he thinks are best and sends them from above. I am grateful for your kind support, the ways you show you care. For the thoughtfulness you've so often shown and the warmness you gladly share. When I've needed you, Mom, on dark, cloudy days, you've always been there for me. I can only hope I've been there for you. If I could choose a mom, I'd surely want you.

Love always, the girl you stuck Velcro on and didn't let get away.

17

Sister Betty and My Favorite Nieces and Nephews

Natalie and Jan Storm with Betty Morrill

FOR MOST OF THE years of our annual vacation gatherings my sister (Aunt Betty to the rest of the family) joined us, often along with daughters Jan and Jeanne, sometimes with sons Rick and Ron and their wives, and especially in later years, her granddaughter Natalie.

Her presence among us held special significance for me. She was my older sister by six years. When I was little she practically raised me and our younger brother John. At least that's how she always told it.

Actually, Betty was my half-sister, though we never used that term. I didn't even know this—at least the reality never really registered with me—until I was well up in my grade school years. Her father, a ministerial student in Eugene, Oregon, had been killed in an automobile accident when she was only three. Her mother (and mine) married my father when Betty was five. Like many children, I guess, we always differed in relating our version of dynamics in the household where we grew up. She seemed to have a built-in insecurity that nothing could erase. Although Dad formally adopted her and from my perspective always treated her as his own—so much so that I didn't know for years she wasn't his—she never accepted that she was fully accepted. She was surprised, for example, that Dad's will divided his small legacy equally among the three of us. I wasn't surprised at all.

As a child I adored Betty. She was pretty, witty, charming, the life of any party. As a teenager and young single adult, I would drag my friends to her house just to show her off. She raised four delightful children. When her first marriage dissolved—a heartbreaking occurrence to Joy and me, since we loved her husband Dick—she held the rest of the family together. She married again, but this marriage was also unsuccessful. She then remained single.

What made her participation in our annual family gatherings so special to me is that our relationship had often had a touch of tension about it. She never fully approved of her brother's religion. We grew up in the same family and attended the same church, but she remained a seeker all her life, experimenting with various isms.

So throughout our adult lives, she often felt uneasy around her altogether too religious brother. She seemed afraid that at any moment I might burst forth into sermon. I probably did too much bursting forth when I was new to the ministry. Time softened me. Still, she considered me pretty narrow-minded, legalistic. She isn't the only one who's held that opinion! And yet, she made it clear that she was proud of me, and I always loved her and loved being with her.

Do you see why I was glad she wanted in on this Velcro family stuff, she who was already in the biological one? She *had* to be my blood sister; she had a choice regarding the Velcro family. She opted in. She became Aunt Betty to the whole group. When she died, she left too big a hole.

I'm really pleased that her daughter Jan and *her* daughter Natalie have stayed with us, not only because they're Aunt Betty's offspring, but because they are special in their own right. We, too, are related by blood, whether we like it or not. But we're also Velcros, voluntarily choosing to stick together. And we like it.

Betty's other children have remained a little more distant. We are on good terms, but they lead busy lives and, though they've all dropped in on our family vacations, they did so as if looking on from a safe distance. When their mother died, they didn't return. Our loss.

18

Tillamook Gets the Last Word

THERE ARE A FEW more Tillamook people you should know about. I've written about Brad and Gretchen Jacob and their offspring. I haven't mentioned that before we became friends Joy and I already enjoyed our friendship with Brad's parents, *Ted and Linda Jacob*. That one started when I was in high school. Linda was two years ahead of me. She was a very popular, pretty, and cool. Even her last name was—*McCool*.[1] I tried my best to get her to pay attention to me. I was pretty awkward about it. Linda in later years confessed she thought I didn't like her. She misinterpreted my warped sense of humor—not the last person to do so, I have to admit.

Anyway, she went for an older man. I didn't know Ted well when I was in high school, but I did know his younger brother, Ken, an outstanding student and athlete. When I got to know Ted, I was equally impressed. Ted followed his father into mink farming, in fact served as the president of the national mink farmers' association. (Brad followed in his father's footsteps until, when America's mink business pretty much dried up, he turned to contracting, using the skills he had learned from George Widmer.) So for years the older Jacobs were our friends; then after the all-family vacations began and we regularly invaded Brad and Gretchen's farm, they joined in. Fortunately, when the Velcros gathered on the younger Jacob farm, Brad's parents often came for an evening or two of campfire fun. On more than one occasion they provided the meal—for example, fresh ocean salmon

---

1. I almost wrote "How cool is that?" But enough's enough!

roasted on the campfire. And in a gesture we'll never forget, they opened their home and garden for the wedding of Candy and Michael Ohanessian.[2]

Loretta Green is one of those quiet, selfless presences who just seem to "be there" in the background until one day you realize she had become one of the inner circle without any fanfare whatsoever. We first got to know her when George Widmer somehow invited our whole gang to her house for dinner. She also made her spare bedroom available whenever we needed it. Then she joined us at the evening campfire.

In time we learned more of her story. Loretta's a widow, a little older than I am. She qualifies for membership, because she has lived with more than her share of family dysfunction. You wouldn't know it though, from her upbeat demeanor. We've been especially happy to learn that she's still close to the elder Jacobs and to George Widmer. They usually have lunch together at least once a week. Our older friends are looking out for one another!

I wish *Jon and Beth Cummings* had been able to vacation more with us. Beth is George and JoAnn Widmer's daughter. Like so many in our lives, they just seemed to "be there," right out on the edge of the circle, standing by but never intruding. On a couple of Tillamook vacations Jon rounded up two or three boatloads of us and we went crabbing, checking his crab pots for the latest catch—which we then ate for dinner. There's nothing better than Oregon's Dungeness crabs. Unless its fresh clams, which we also ate after the Widmer clan took us clamming.

The rest of the family didn't get to be with us in those precious moments we had together with the Widmers as JoAnn was dying. But Joy and I were there. The love of the Widmer children and sons- and daughters-in-law filled JoAnn's heart and the whole house as they all cared for their mother and father through this peaceful but nonetheless painful transition.

There's almost no place to bring this section of the book to a close, because like biological families, a Velcro one goes on from generation to generation. The Velcro gene seems to be inheritable. We see our kids and

---

2. There's a little more to the story. Ted also served as the wedding videographer. He devoted so much footage to the flowers that the tape ran out about halfway through the ceremony. Well, they were indeed beautiful flowers. The bedroom door at the Ohanessians is still adorned by the cardboard "Honeymoon Suite" sign that Brad and Gretchen Jacobs hung on their bridal tent.

grandkids continuing the tradition of reaching out and bringing in. Grandson Nick, for example, frequently brought his friend Tim home all through high school. And after high school. To this day Tim is like another brother to Nick, a married brother with five children whom we all got to know at—where else?—family vacation. And so it goes.

Part 2

How Do You Build a Velcro Family?

Fourteen Principles

Here's the short answer: We don't know. We didn't start out to build one. It's as if we woke up one day and discovered our family had grown really big without any plan. It just *became.*

I caught on to the full meaning of *Velcro family* around the vacation campfire several years ago. We've never actually structured our weeks together, but a pattern has emerged over time. After dinner we migrate to the bonfire, where after small conversations in twos or threes, the general storytelling just kind of begins, often after Brian and Gretchen and Nick bring out their guitars. They then lead us in some singing that's of, shall we say, rather mixed quality.

By now we've almost memorized some of the tales. They're dragged out by popular demand, year after year. There are also new ones. Each year one or several of our accident-prone gang recount their latest embarrassing stunts; they then endure the predictable, good-natured ridicule that follows. We all look forward to these evenings; sometimes they are magic.

In the year in question, though, I took over. Some visitors had joined us. I thought we should explain ourselves to them, since a Velcro family, while not unique, is pretty rare, so for the visitors' sake I asked the "regulars" to tell them "how you got into our Velcro family and what keeps you here." One by one around the circle they recounted their histories with us. It quickly became evident that in our family, as the scripture says, "There is none righteous, no, not one." We have had everything: alcoholism, drug addiction, criminality and jail time, divorce, bankruptcy, joblessness, depression, suicide. We openly spoke of misadventures, of stumbling and sinning, of feeling lost and being found, and of somehow discovering ourselves in the embrace of this inclusive, nonjudgmental, genuinely loving family.

And me? As the *paterfamilias* I thought, quite presumptuously, I suppose, *This must be how God feels when God contemplates his own large, dysfunctional family. He loves them and he won't, if he can help it, give up one of them.* Because there isn't a person here *I* would willingly give up, I realized. We *are* a family. We stick together, no matter what. Like Velcro.

So, while I can't give you a three- or five-step formula for starting a Velcro family, I can and do regularly give thanks for letting me be part of one.

Perhaps a clue to what happened to us can be found in a practice I learned early in my work as a pastor. As the church grew, it quickly became apparent I couldn't take care of all the people myself. There were just too many. So I adopted what I came to call a "Cupid Ministry." Not a very spiritual title, I admit, but an accurate one. It simply means I introduced people to one another and helped them fall in love with each other. Not romantically or sexually, obviously, but with the love of the Lord. My goal was to help them become important to each other so each would always "be there" for the other. As a pastor I knew my days were limited; the time would inevitably come for me to leave the congregation. I wanted them to continue to be solidly related to each other after I was gone.

That has happened in our Velcro family. I can't be what I'd like to be for each of the members, but what I have tried to do, either directly or indirectly, is help them become—and remain—important to each other, even when Grandma and Grandpa are no longer with them. That matters more to me now than ever, since that inevitable day draws ever closer.

So you see, while I can't tell you how to build a Velcro family I do have some opinions about what it takes to hold one together. Here is my list. You understand, we're such a diverse—and strongly opinionated—group that probably no two of us would give you the same list. This is mine—offered with Grandma's consent.

1. Your Love Must Be for Real

At the risk of belaboring the obvious, I must start with this one: We have learned that *loving* isn't the same as *liking*. If you'd interview all the Velcros, they would admit there are others in our family whose company they don't particularly enjoy all the time. That's OK. Liking isn't the requirement. Loving is. If you don't want the best for your "adoptive" brothers and sisters, you probably won't stick around. If you will only enter into a long-term relationship with people you totally approve of, whose ideas and opinions you agree with, whose culture is *your* culture, a large Velcro family will make you very uncomfortable. But if you're willing to first accept and then to learn to care about others who aren't exactly like you, then you just might make it!

I'll have more to say about this requirement in relation to several other suggestions on the following pages. Love has many facets. "I love you" is so easy to say and so hard to do that it must be named first and repeated often. As I am typing these words, in my ears I am hearing the apostle Paul: "*Love is patient and kind; love is not jealous or boastful; it is not arrogant or rude. Love does not insist on its own way; it is not irritable or resentful; it does not rejoice at wrong, but rejoices in the right. Love bears all things, believes all things, hopes all things, endures all things. Love never ends.*"[1]

That about sums it up. The love that holds a Velcro family together can't rely on blood ties or rules or implicit expectations or extrinsic rewards. Membership can't get you a job or guarantee a good retirement or somehow enhance your reputation. It's not something to be used and then, when no longer needed, tossed away. It's not something you somehow stumble into and just as easily stumble out of. It's not a short-term fling; it's a long-term commitment. It's what the Biblical *agape* love is like. *Love never ends.*

2. You Apply Generous Heaps of Grace and Forgiveness

Our Velcro family didn't teach me this lesson. I learned it decades ago, early in my ministry years. A pastor becomes, if only by default, a counselor, like it or not. When they are in trouble, people—whether they are regular church attenders or just have a vague memory of or connection to a church—turn to the pastor. Pastors are supposed to know how to fix marriages, how to mend broken hearts, how to hold a family together. They are expected to give good advice on a wide range of subjects. And they're cheap. Free, actually. So when I was still a young man, before I knew enough to even pretend to be a counselor, I became one. At the same time I also became a student of the people who sought my advice. I quickly caught on that I could do nothing unless they'd do the one thing they were most determined *not* to do. If they couldn't or more accurately *wouldn't* forgive, they were not going to get well and the broken relationship would not be saved.

My parents taught me this lesson, though they didn't know it. Over their nineteen years together the love they must have once felt for each other gave way to coldness, disapproval, and eventual disgust. They finally

---

1. 1 Cor 13:4–8 (*Revised Standard Version*).

wanted nothing to do with each other. The grace they heard about in church, they somehow couldn't summon when it was most needed.

I initially applied the lesson their tragedy taught me to marriages—my parents', my parishioners', my own. Only gradually did I grasp the wider implications: This principle isn't limited to marriage. You can't hold *any* long-term relationship together without grace and forgiveness. I examined my own friendships. Nobody has better friends than I do. Yet I had to confess there wasn't one in which I hadn't messed up in some way. And, if I dared to look closely enough, there wasn't one in which I couldn't find something about *them* to complain about. Do you think I was never offended—or offensive?

Mike Prior illustrated this principle for me more than thirty years ago, when he was Central Christian's executive pastor. He was chatting with a staff member of another church who was bemoaning the turnover of personnel there, especially among youth ministers. It wasn't surprising, since that senior pastor had a reputation as a demanding, impatient boss. Mike's response, as he reported later, was something like this: "Hmmm, that's interesting. At Central we've all had our bad years, but we just hang on to each other 'til we get through them."

What made his statement stick was this: Mike didn't say we all have our bad days, or bad weeks, or even bad months. He said *years*! He was right. I could have named each of our ministers and pointed out their struggles, their victories and defeats, those moments when they stood on tiptoes, and those when they could hardly stand up. And they could have told their tales of their boss's disasters. Yet it was as if we'd taken some kind of secret pledge that we wouldn't turn on one another. We weren't just co-workers. We had become friends. And friends forgive and hang on to each other *in spite of*.

So do Velcro families.

3. You Keep the Doors Open—for Coming and Going

One of the most painful moments in parenting comes when the teenagers leave home, either happily because college or career beckons, or unhappily because household tensions have grown so severe they just want out. So they leave. Usually parents understand that such parting is inevitable, and no permanent damage is done. Not infrequently, though, the parents slam the door to keep the—in their opinion—erring child at home, safe, under control. Or, in total exasperation, they lock the door after they're gone.

Mistake. The more difficult the parents make the parting, the more difficult they make the return.

For years I've quipped, "Here's the problem with being a parent. You do everything you can to help your child grow up to be independent. And you succeed." This is your goal, of course. But this is one victory that's guaranteed to hurt, at least a little.

At the heart of this matter is control. There's a reason pop psychologists talk so freely about "control issues." Most of us not only want to run our own lives but we also want to run others': bosses over employees, parents over children, friends over friends, spouse over spouse—everybody over *somebody*.

A lesson this Velcro family taught me early on, especially at our annual all-family vacation, was that I simply could not get everybody together for anything. My initial goal was more ambitious: I wanted us all to be together for *everything*. Let's eat together, gather around the bonfire together, pray together, go on our excursions together, and for certain let's not let anything interfere with our vacation week. Let's all be there every year—together. And let's do everything we do—together.

It just doesn't work that way. There was/is no way to corral everybody.

I had to apply another lesson I learned about marriage from pastoral counseling—and from paying attention to popular music. Listen carefully to love songs. They're often about how much the singer needs the one he/she loves, how she/he can't live without the other. This sentiment sells recordings. But it kills marriages, friendships, families—Velcro families.

What I learned is this: marriages (and other relationships) based on how much *I need you* are neurotic; misery guaranteed. Healthy marriages (and other relationships) are based not so much on *how I need you* but on *how I want you but if necessary can still have a healthy life without you*.

Thus the Velcro family. We don't really need each other. All of us can get through life without having to belong to this motley assembly of misfits. But all of us make a priority of being together because we *want* to. And we can leave any time we want to. Some of us have been family for decades now—Jeff and I have been surrogate son and father to each other for more than fifty-five years. We could have walked away from each other at any time. There was a period during Jeff's drinking years, in fact, when it appeared that we might not get through it together—but neither of us let go. That's the secret—we *chose* not to let go.

And that's the secret with everyone else in the family. We may not *need*, but we certainly *want*, each other.

4. The Biological Core Must Be Willing

This essential deserves a chapter of its own. Whenever Joy and I try to explain how our Velcro family works, we start with our biological kids, because without them this couldn't have happened.

We raised three socially active children. Even as preschoolers, they could be found playing with the neighbor kids or school or church friends. At home, though, they acted more like introverts. Because their father has always been a noisy little man, people have always assumed we had a noisy household. Paradoxically, it was because we were so socially active, we seemed, without ever really talking about it, to want our home to be a quiet place. It became a haven for regrouping our resources, I suppose, gathering up strength to charge out into society again.

So we took pride, Mom and I, as our kids found their ways in society, in Tennessee, in Indiana, and in their teen years in Arizona. Thanks to their mother they enjoyed our home's Open Door Policy. They were free to invite their friends over whenever they wanted. This was especially true in Arizona, when there always seemed to be extra teenagers hanging around. We loved it. Interestingly, it was the visitors who provided the noise. Left to ourselves, all five of us enjoyed peace and quiet.

I already reported on that brief period when we had five teenagers living in at once. The two extra were really Kim's doing. She's responsible for Brian. And she was responsible for Rosa, our Ecuadoran exchange student. In Indiana she invited her friend Kelly Wilmoth to move in for awhile. It just seemed the natural thing to do.

Candy's and Lane's friends were also frequent visitors, although they didn't recruit future Velcros the way Kim did. What all three children shared, however, was their readiness to make room for any newcomer. They never expressed—at least to us parents—resentment that someone else might be taking their place. Because of course nobody *could* take their place. Just as Joy was always able to stretch a meal to feed whoever appeared at mealtime, so the kids could stretch the living space so no one felt excluded.

5. Mother's Patience Must Be Almost Infinite

I probably should have named this characteristic the Number One Essential. Since Dear Old Dad was at work most of the time, it fell to Joy to set the household tone. The tone was, unfailingly, hospitable. We've mused about this in later years, since Joy and her twin brother, Dan, grew up in a tight-knit, self-sufficient home. They didn't have overnight guests (except, perhaps, the occasional drifter her preacher father would invite home for dinner and a place to sleep). In my teen years my mother wasn't comfortable with guests, especially overnight ones. By then my parents' marriage was undeniably in trouble, so I didn't feel free to invite. But Kim and Candy and Lane did. And they did because of their mother's openness.

Joy says she learned to practice hospitality because she married me. I say I felt free to bring people home because I married her. She simply never said no. She could whip up meals out of almost nothing, especially toward the end of the month. A little more water in the soup, a few more leftovers in the stew. So the Lawson table always had room for one more. Or several more.

The kids caught her spirit of hospitality.

This Velcro family would never have been built without her.

6. "Group Think" Is Verboten

I wouldn't have thought to list this principle until recently, although we've implicitly applied it from the beginning.

From the first sentences of this account you've been aware that the author is a minister. That means he subscribes to the basic tenets of the Christian religion. And that means that some people will be attracted because of his faith while others will be turned off for the same reason. That's how religion works, I'm afraid. The Christian faith preaches unity while sometimes fostering division.

When I was a young pastor and father, I pretty much took it for granted that any child of mine would follow in my footsteps. I cherished the privilege of baptizing each one in turn; the pride I took in them when they participated in the church's children's and then youth activities was all too evident, I'm afraid. So in spite of what I had observed in other families, I was emotionally unprepared for the day when all three in turn declared in their own inimitable fashions, that they were not going to follow this or that part of my teachings any longer. "Don't take it personally, Dad. This isn't about you," they assured me, trying to ease the pain. But naturally I did take it personally.

Well, I had to get over it. It was a lesson I needed to learn. To repeat myself: We had raised our children to be independent—and we had succeeded, with all three. Genuinely independent people don't merely mimic what someone else thinks, even when that someone is Dad or Mom. They reserve and deserve the right to make up their own minds. That's what our three did. They didn't come to the same conclusions, but they did get to their conclusions on their own. Even when we were disagreeing in those days, I had to admit I was proud of their integrity.

When Lane was a student at Northern Arizona University in Flagstaff, he called home to let us know he and his girlfriend had moved in together. You understand—he was telling (not asking!) his preacher father that he was deliberately doing something he knew his father would disapprove of. He got the expected response. After he'd listened to me sputter for a while he retorted, "But Dad, you always taught us to be honest."

"Not *this* honest," I nearly shouted, then handed the phone to his mother. Now what kind of a response was that, anyway? If not *this* honest, what did I expect him to say? Did I want him to lie? No, I wanted him not to have done what he'd done. But it was too late for that.

And the truth is—I was proud of his honesty, proud that he wasn't sneaking around, and proud that he cared enough about his parents and felt secure enough in his relationship with us to talk to us directly.

All three also respected us enough to talk over their religious feelings and thoughts and doubts. I think they felt safe, that we wouldn't reject them when they disagreed with us—even though they probably also knew it would take Dad awhile to come around.

I've talked about our biological kids and their religious differences as an introduction to talking about the Velcro kids. You've probably already guessed it, but let me be explicit: Religious agreement has not been a requisite for membership in this family. If you'd interview each of us individually, you might be surprised to discover that we are all over the board, the spectrum reaching from the religious professionals on the one pole to practical atheists on the other. We just tacitly agree that this family will be a safe place, where unconditional love is a fact and not just a concept. I've often quoted a saying a fellow minister gave me many years ago. We were talking about friendship, *our* friendship, when he quoted this gem. It wasn't original with him, but I can't remember where he got it. "A friend," he said, "is someone in whose presence I can think aloud tentatively without being held to my tentative conclusions."

Our Velcro family consists of friends "who can think aloud tentatively . . ."

This essential ingredient gets tested from time to time. To be candid, President Trump has put us to the toughest test. This most divisive of politicians has not only fostered discord on the national scene but has managed to do the same in our family. We have devout Trumpites who are pretty much persuaded the man can do no wrong; we also have committed anti-Trumpites who are equally persuaded he can do no right. I've thought more than once about America's Civil War, when families were split down the middle over the issues of slavery and secession. I used to wonder about those families; now I've seen how easily such a division could have ripped them asunder.

Which is what led me to include this characteristic of a successful Velcro family: "Group think" is not our goal; in fact, insistence on it is forbidden. That is, we have agreed that for the sake of family unity, we will not insist that *everybody* has to agree with *me*. We will accentuate the positive, we will give thanks for each other's virtues even as we question their opinions. And we will not, we absolutely will not, let go of each other. There must be some place in this world where unqualified love rules, and that place is our family.

My father taught me this fundamental when I was a boy. He was an independent grocer in a small town. His older son was a talkative, often insensitive child who sometimes expressed his opinions a little too freely with the customers. For the most part, Dad enjoyed these conversations. Except sometimes. When I got a little too lippy, asserting my unassailable opinions a little too dogmatically—because I was right, you see—he'd march me back to the store's walk-in cooler where we could talk privately—and get to the point quickly, since it was cold in there. There he explained—yet again—the limit to which I could go. Honest disagreement politely expressed was one thing. Any hint of disrespect was forbidden.

Two topics were off limit, he insisted: politics and religion. People take their political views and their religious practices *very* seriously. They are not to be argued with. If I got carried away, he could lose customers.

Point taken. Point applied in this family, also. Strong opinions abound among us. For some people, attacking a political or religious position is tantamount to attacking the person. When the atmosphere becomes too charged, people either explode and attack or they retreat. Neither reaction is acceptable. We have learned, for the most part, "to live and let live," tolerating what we must, hanging on to each other no matter what.

Joy likes to relate her favorite illustration of this principle. "When I acquired a stepsister," Joy has told her friends from time to time, "I quickly learned that my new sister loved to argue about any religious subject she had heard about recently. I chose not to get involved, so just listened. About five years into this stepsister problem, she said to me, 'Joy, I used to think you weren't very religious, but I've come to realize that you live your religion and I just bullshit a lot.' I couldn't have said it better myself. Love speaks louder than words."

7. Rituals Create Memories . . . and Anticipation

Other contributors to this book and I have already talked a lot about our annual all-family vacation. Nothing has proved more important in holding us together than this yearly event. We plan our vacations from work around the date (always July, either the third or the fourth week—except for our two all-family cruises, and those we planned two years in advance to give everyone time to reserve the unusual date). Sometimes other obligations necessarily interfere (school or college schedules, financial pressures, inadequate vacation time, etc.), but we make our all-family week a priority.

While Joy and I lived in Mesa the vacation week was a highlight every year, but not yet the necessity it subsequently became. That's because everybody (or almost everybody) could come to Grandma's house for Thanksgiving, Christmas, and even Easter. We'd be there, since as a pastor I couldn't get away, especially for Christmas and Easter holidays. We stayed in Mesa, but whoever wanted to come "home for the holidays" knew where to find us. And they came.

But in 1999 Grandma moved to California. Then she and Grandpa wandered around America in their motor home for a year-and-a-half before settling in Payson again. Then moved again to Tennessee again. Finally they gave up settling and went on the loose all over the world from 2016 to 2020. In other words, the family couldn't count on going to Grandma's house anymore. Instead, the grandparents descended on the descendants for the holidays: with the Thompsons in Missouri and the Ohanessians in Australia or England or someplace else. Now, though, with the Arbaughs settling back in Arizona where the Philipses and Reynolds and Domkes and Brian already are, the balance is tipping toward the Southwest, so the grandparents have the additional option of Arizona—and maybe even

Colorado. But the reliable constant is the all-family vacation; it remains a priority somewhere every summer.

What makes these holidays and vacations so important is not just our being together, as essential as that is, but that when we are together, especially for the vacation week, we can practice our rituals. There will be

- A big all-family meal each evening, with everyone assigned to kitchen duty (preparing, cooking, serving, cleaning up) one night of the week.

- A bonfire if possible at the close of each day.

- S'mores for the children—of all ages

- Storytelling. Some of the favorites have grown very old but not frail. They've been repeated for lo these many years—but seem to grow more robust if a little less believable with each retelling.

- Group activities. High on the list of desirables are white-water rafting (with its enthusiastic wars between the rafts), spelunking (if there's a cave nearby), crabbing and clamming (if we're in Tillamook and Jon Cummings is available to take us), ice cream excursions to the Tillamook County Creamery, the ladies' tea (again, in Tillamook), soaring (with its attending airsickness), playing in the sand at the beach, skeet shooting at the Jacob farm, making and enjoying homemade apple cider, visiting a "robot" dairy farm, going to the theater (movie and live) as a group, invading and taking over local restaurants, church, and more. It doesn't matter so much what we do but who we are doing it with.

These are not required group activities, but optional. Just about everybody opts in, though. Some of us (Jeff comes to mind, and George, and . . .) can't join in the fun with as much gusto as we once applied, but we get a different kind of kick now. We've become the audience for the younger, more energetic ones who've taken our place. We old-timers have migrated from the playing field to the grandstand. Cheering is almost as much fun as competing. Almost.

Several times I've mentioned my satisfaction in being the eldest pastor in the family. What an honor it is to preside at family weddings, ordinations, baptisms, birth celebrations. And funerals. Yes, even funerals bring a kind of joy, when the one you are honoring has meant so much to the family.

All these events are rites of passage, opportunities for further bonding and expressions of love. And almost invariably they elicit promises. We part from one another already anticipating the next get-together. Some old hymns say it for us: "God be with you 'til we meet again," and "Blessed be the tie that binds . . ."

8. You Make Room for Spaces in the Togetherness

As everybody knows, family reunions can sometimes be fraught with tension. They provide the sometimes hilarious, sometimes tragic plots for movies; playwrights construct award-winning dramas about them. Ours have not always been tension free. I've been the most uptight of all, especially in the early years when I was still trying to be in control. Which was crazy. For nine years I led a couple of organizations at the same time, a megachurch in Arizona, and a small university in California. When people asked me how I managed the two jobs, I had a couple of stock answers. The first: "It's easy. Wherever they want me, I'm at the other place." After I retired from the church and had only the university to run, I learned that my quip wasn't a joke. It was easier to administer both than just one. Now they could find me!

The second stock response was this: "Oh, I'm in charge. I'm just not in control." There's a difference. I was able to survive those nine years because, while everybody recognized that I was in charge, it was also clear that I couldn't be in control of everything. In fact, I controlled almost nothing. The church and campus ran most smoothly when I spelled out the parameters, then got out of the way and let the responsible parties do their jobs.

Thus the Velcro family. The grandparent generation (Joy and I) are nominally in charge. We're treated respectfully, even if we must seem pretty much in our dotage to the rising generations. We are consulted, considered, even politely listened to on occasion. But we're never in control of these independent individuals we call our kids—and grandkids—and great grandkids.

Another lesson from my past comes to mind here. In my master's program at Reed College I took a psychology course on motivation, paying particular attention to what motivates adolescent boys. I've forgotten most of what the professor had to say then—and psychological theories have continued to evolve so that much of what I learned is now passé, but one lesson has stuck for a lifetime. A study had been made of boys and their fathers. The goal was to discover the best kind of father for raising a highly motivated son. The answer, surprising at least to me, was "a sea-going captain." Why? Because the captain was himself a highly motivated man who was a model of accomplishment, but who wasn't around on a day-to-day basis to stifle or overly control his son's forays into independence. The son could admire his father from afar. That was enough.

What that means for Joy and me is pretty apparent, isn't it? Our first contribution to the Velcro family is to remain active as long as we can, living out what we believe, continuing to grow ourselves even as we encourage the rest of the family—grandparents, parents, children—to keep on learning and developing, without getting in the way. In other words, to root for one another and the rest of the family in developing like Jesus "in wisdom and stature and in favor with God and man."

How do we apply this principle, the grandmother and I? We cherish our times together and try to make our getting together happen as often as possible. But we also attempt to keep a respectful distance, trying not to smother or discourage, stifling our natural impulse to take over. We try, as in a good marriage and cherished friendship, to guarantee there'll be spaces in our togetherness.

9. Forget about Perfection in Behavior and Total Agreement in Opinions

I've probably said enough about this essential already. Let me just add a few more words. I'm a preacher, you'll remember. I arrange my thoughts into three points, as I was taught: You tell 'em what you're gonna tell 'em, then you tell 'em, then you tell 'em what you done told 'em. So here I'm telling you what I done told you.

It's another abiding lesson from my ministry years. In undergraduate Bible college I took the required class in homiletics (the science of preaching). We had to memorize a definition of preaching. I've forgotten most of it by now, but one phrase has stuck with me. We preach, the definition asserts, "with a view to persuasion." That is, we aren't speaking just to entertain and certainly not to show off nor even primarily to teach, but to convince our auditors to our own point of view. When the sermon's over and the last hymn has been sung, the goal is that our parishioners will leave the service thinking, "You know, the preacher is right. I agree with him. In fact, I'm determined to do what he says about it. I'm persuaded."

By that definition, I often felt myself a failure. You'll remember I couldn't always persuade my own children. Or, for that matter, on some subjects not even their mother! She insists on doing her own thinking, thank you. Now here's the deal: I've preached what I believe. I'm not an actor who, as Shakespeare says, "struts and frets his part upon a stage and then is heard no more . . . full of sound and fury but signifying nothing." Nope. I've done some strutting, no doubt; there might even have been occasional moments of fury. But I wasn't acting. I was in earnest. I used all the oratorical tools at my disposal to teach persuasively. But I couldn't always persuade.

As in the church, so in the family. I can huff and puff but I can't blow the resisting doors down.

This demanding definition of the preacher's task could have been really discouraging. It could have driven me from my calling, because it sets a goal beyond my reach. It didn't, though. Instead of abandoning my calling, I abandoned the definition.

May I return to that phone call with Lane? It was apparent he and his girlfriend Kim were going to live together, regardless of Dad's disapproval. It was a crisis moment. I was so shaken I spoke to the elders at their next meeting. Without going into personal details, I asked them to take some time evaluating my ministry. "I'm damaged goods," I confessed that much. I couldn't present a picture of the perfect family—and certainly not of the perfect preacher-father. Should I resign?

The elders met without me to soberly evaluate whether I should hang it up. They reached a conclusion—which they didn't bother to tell me about for several days, while I waited on pins and needles. If they had said the word, I would have resigned. Then at church on Sunday, as I was talking with some people in the hall, Rex Dernovich, the chairman of the elders, paused briefly as he breezed by. "Oh, by the way . . ." he said. By the way!! I felt my ministry was in crisis, and he treated my situation as something quite "by the way"? "By the way," he said. "We decided you aren't perfect, but don't quit."

That was it. I've replayed that brief moment again and again. Because Rex was right: It was *by the way*. They'd known all along that their pastor was a flawed man. Nothing new here. But they'd followed me anyway. They also admitted that they had their own family problems, several of which I'd helped them through. If I could accept them with their flaws, they reasoned, they could accept me with mine. What they were after was not a perfect model of a pastor, but an imperfect human being who was struggling along with them to follow Jesus, who long ago taught us how to put up with, even to love, the disagreeing and the disagreeable among us—including ourselves.

It took me awhile, but I think I finally learned that this lesson is one of the essentials in Velcro family living. We're all pretty messed up. Put us in the same room and lock the doors and it won't be long before chaos might break out. People could get hurt. Relationships will be strained if not severed.

That's why we don't lock the door. As I said above, we leave it open, granting plenty of space in our togetherness, so we will be able to tolerate when we can't persuade. And in time, that toleration can blossom into appreciation and the appreciation into affection.

10. No One Owns the Membership Roll

You've already caught on to this essential. It took me a long time to. I certainly didn't think of it before we started to be a Velcro family.

I call it "Velcros Velcroing." You've seen those old sepia-colored pictures from the early days of photography. There in the center are Grandma and Grandpa, stiffly posing for the camera, attired in their finest. They're surrounded by their offspring. And their offspring's offspring. And the in-laws. And probably a distant cousin or two and the next-door neighbor thrown in for good measure. You wonder whether they all know each other. And who was left out.

In November 2019 a group photo was shot at a Velcro minireunion at the Arbaugh's house in Arizona. Someone shouted for a picture. So we posed. It was only part of our Velcro family, those who could be there for Central Christian's sixtieth anniversary celebration. When I studied the photo later, several things impressed me about the people in the picture:

1. We are all ages, from the oldest (Grandma Joy and me) to the youngest (Estin, six).

2. Only our daughter Kim and Joy and I are related by blood.

3. No one—including the grandparents—knew everybody else.

4. Some had never been with the Velcro family before, like the woman who had sold the Arbaughs their new house. They invited her for the

evening. Brian was acquainted with her through his real estate work. No one else had ever met her. Years from now people will wonder who she is.

5. Debbie and Mark Hollenbach are in the picture. They were invited because Debbie had all our kids in her Salt of the Earth youth choir years ago and her pastor husband, Mark, had worked with several of us on the Central Christian staff. Many present that evening didn't know them; those who did were very glad they came.

6. Riley was there, also. We were so glad she came. Her mother Laurie, Patti's best friend, had died of cancer just two days earlier. She needed family now more than ever. She remembered her first vacation week with our Velcro family when she was about four years old. When Patti invited her to join us at the Arbaughs, she knew a warm welcome awaited her.

In other words, it was a typical Velcro family photo. And the Arbaughs were simply honoring the tradition: Any member can invite anyone else to join us at any time. Over the years many accepted the invitation, came for a gathering or two, and then disappeared. A kind of "self-selection" takes place. The truth is, Velcro family living isn't for everyone. It's kind of like church: "Whosoever will may come," and "Many are called, few chosen." Velcro stickiness doesn't work on everyone.

That's because not everybody fits. There are no rules to be obeyed, no tests to be passed, but somehow someone just seems to belong—or not. For one thing, you can't wear your feelings on your sleeve. You can't expect everybody to drop everything to make you feel welcome. Some of the initiative has to be yours. Back to the early example of Brian, who just wouldn't go away. Forty years later we're glad he wouldn't. Anyone can leave at any time. We just hope they won't.

I wrote part of this book while on board the Celebrity *Constellation* on our way from Rome to Dubai to visit friends Stuart and Dana Telford (and their children Jack and Millie), whom Brian and I married in Mesa about fourteen years ago. The ship stopped in Abu Dhabi for a day. Joy and I mostly spent that day in a taxi, visiting the Grand Mosque ("the world's largest"), the Presidential Palace, the Emirates Hotel, and other examples of what free-flowing oil money can buy.

Sameel, our congenial driver, had been living in the Emirates for seventeen years, driving long hours in order to support his wife and three children back home in Kerala, India. One interesting fact we learned about his adopted country was this: Sameel can never really belong here. United Arab Emirates citizenship is forever closed to him. Only 20 percent of UAE's population are citizens. The rest are foreigners like him; they are allowed to live in the country because somebody has to do the work. Sameel can remain on a renewable visa until in his sixties. He stays because he can't earn as good a living in India. But he has no hope of ever gaining an Emirates passport. The population's classes (castes) are forever set.

That's exactly the opposite of a genuine Velcro family. Naturally blood came first. That is, in the beginning we were a family unit whose children share their parents' DNA. Chronology accounts for that difference. But unlike in the UAE, blood descent alone does not define citizenship in this family. On these pages I've used *Velcro* as a noun, adjective, and even verb form to describe the "naturalized" citizens who weren't born into the family but who have all the rights, privileges, and perquisites appertaining thereto (to employ some verbiage I used when granting diplomas as a university president).

We didn't invent the label. We were in Australia one year when I was visiting professor of a small college in Sydney. Joy was explaining to Iris Armstrong, our hostess, how our family operates. She exclaimed, "Why, they are your *Velcro* children." That was exactly the right word. In our Velcro family we just stick together—like Velcro. And there's no caste system.

11. You Remember and Practice the Principle of Stewardship

Now I *am* going to sound like a preacher. A fundamental Christian tenet is this one: We are stewards of the abilities, experiences, and opportunities God gives us. In the church all the members are assumed to have spiritual gifts, and those gifts are expected to be offered to the church for the good of the body as a whole. It's through these gifted people and their gifts the church fulfills its commission for the benefit of the world. Example: I preach. I'm not good for much else. But since this is the one thing I *can* do, this one thing I *must* do. An essential assignment for the leader of a church, though, is not just doing what he or she can do personally, but also helping the members do what *they* can.

That's how a Velcro family works. I'm the noisy leader of this clan, but as I wrote earlier, without Joy's quiet support and "mothering" the Velcro family wouldn't have made it. And without our biological kids' welcoming spirit, others would have been frozen out. So in turn all members of the family bring what they have so the whole body (Velcro family) works.

Here's what's expected: If you have toys, the whole family enjoys them. Example: For the first decades together we all relied on Jeff to share his toys, and even his and Joan's home. He had the boats, the jet skis, the water skis, the Jeep, the kayaks, the motor home, etc. And he freely provided them for the rest of us. Then later his Velcro son Derek brought along *his* boat, and we all moved into his places in Canby and LaPine for a vacation week.

I'm talking about more than just *things*.

If you are musical, the whole family sings along with you. (Brian and Gretchen and Nick and their guitars come to mind.)

And if you can sing, the group clamors to hear your rendition of "Blowin' in the Wind" or "The Rose"—and even if you can't sing all that well, we'll still demand your rendition of "The Gooey Duck Song."

If you can cook, you can't keep the whole family from enjoying your gifts.

If you can write or act, especially if you are young, you'll be the camp-fire entertainment.

If you ride a motorcycle, you bring along extra helmets because on this vacation, "You'll Never (Ride) Alone."

If you own a farm with an empty cabin on it, you won't be able to keep us away from it, since it's a perfect rendezvous spot for our annual vacation.

If you have friends we can take advantage of, we'll be happy to let you put the arm on them for their spare bedroom, their crab boat, their smoked salmon, etc.

If you think you don't have anything special, sit quietly and let the performers perform for you. Engaged listening, too, is a gift.

And so it goes. What becomes clear over time is that those who contribute most to the whole family have the strongest sense of belonging. Again it's like church. Persons who remain on the periphery never quite "get" what church is all about. And those who hide on the edges of a family, taking what's offered but contributing little, never quite "get" what family is all about, either.

12. You Prioritize the Children and Respect the Elderly

This is another item I wouldn't have listed in our earlier years together. I had to grow old to gain this perspective. Our Velcro children have always been important to us. But then came those years when the first generation of children had grown and been gone for a while. They left an empty spot around the campfire. Family vacation just didn't seem the same without them. That emptiness has now been filled. Some are coming back after being gone for a year or more. And another generation of little ones has arrived. They are our best entertainment, our source of hope. They are the elastic bonds that will hold the family together when the grandparent generation is gone. Just watching them be themselves is all we ask of children when they are little. As they grow older they'll pick up their share of the chores. They'll learn to love as they are loved. Then it'll be their turn to cheer on the children—their children.

Another reason I wouldn't have included this requirement in our earlier years is that I was younger then, more active, and able to participate in everything. Now I'm not. We already had an older generation, even before Joy and I were in it. We were grateful to have George and JoAnn Widmer with us, and Aunt Faye and her sister Lorraine, Loretta Green, my brother and sister-in-law John and Sharon, Aunt Betty, and more. We welcomed them gladly. They were part of the family, always treated with respect.

Now Joy and I have joined their ranks—and we are granted the same consideration. Oh, sometimes the teasing comes right to the brink of disrespect, but never over it. Teasing is our family's love language, and we old-timers enjoy it. It does in fact convey that love.

13. Seize the Joy of "Being There for Each Other"

You've caught on by now that developing a Velcro family is absolutely *not* about one-way giving. Joy and I have given something to each one of the family. But that pales in comparison with what we have received. Reciprocity governs all our relationships.

This brings me at long last to tell you of the single event Joy and I point to as a—perhaps *the*—defining moment in the formalizing of our Velcro family. It's when we decided we needed—*wanted*—to guarantee this family would get together at least one week a year. The resulting annual vacation has been the single most important commitment that holds us all together.

You've already heard much of the backstory from others in the family. You have my permission to skip this section. It probably seems repetitious. That's because this event in our history was so pivotal. For me this story begins with the much-anticipated motorcycle ride from Arizona to Oregon that never happened. Jeff and Joan's son Shawn was to be married in their hometown, Canby, Oregon. He and Toni asked me to do the honors. As often happens with us, that simple event soon grew bigger than itself. Velcro son Mike and I would take time off from our jobs in Mesa, hop on our bikes and ride over to California where longtime friend Chuck Boatman would join us, and together we three would ride to the Oregon border. There Jeff and Shawn would meet us on their motorcycles. Then the five of us would make our way to Canby for the wedding. Great plan.

But instead, just one month before the wedding I caught a plane to Portland. In place of marrying Shawn to Toni, I conducted Shawn's funeral. He died in a car-motorcycle accident just a few miles from home.

I don't have to tell you how devastated we all were. I feared for Jeff. He had gone through rehab five years earlier. He hadn't touched a drop of alcohol since. If anything could trigger a relapse, Shawn's death would do it. How is it possible to cope with your horrible sense of loss, your regrets, your inevitable self-blaming? Jeff and I spent hours talking. We'd been through some difficulties together before, but nothing like this. Joan could draw on reserves from her family and friends and her strong Christian faith. I was concerned about her, but not worried. But Jeff?

He made it. He didn't take up drink again. He did rely on his faith in God. He showed a maturity and sense of responsibility to Joan and the girls and an openness in our conversations that made it possible for me to return to Arizona convinced that even his son's death would not defeat Jeff. I was proud.

Then it was my turn. Five years later our son, Lane, died. Even worse, he took his own life. You've picked up parts of the story earlier in this book. What matters here is what happened with the four grieving parents. The tables were turned.

Lane had lived in Southern Oregon; we were living in Arizona and California—this was while I was pastor at Central Christian in Mesa and president of Pacific Christian College in Fullerton. Lane had moved to Port Orford and later Brookings in search of purer air, better health. It didn't work out for him. Instead, he felt his body continuing to deteriorate. He'd been fighting neurochemical depression for years, his allergies to petrochemicals triggering dark feelings, a sense of hopelessness. Then a tick did its fatal number on him. Lane contracted Lyme's Disease, a symptom of which is debilitating depression—depression piled on depression. Lane just felt ganged up on. He drove his pickup truck into a favorite spot in the forest near Brookings, attached a hose to its tailpipe, and inhaled.

An Arizona State policeman rapped on our door in Payson at 4:00 a.m. Joy was by herself. Before opening the door she called the police department to be sure he was in fact a policeman. She was alone and not taking chances. He delivered the devastating news. She called nearby friends Rollie and Phyllis Lee. They drove her the hour-and-a-half down the mountain to Mesa so she could tell me in person (I had just returned from California and spent the night in our Mesa condo.)

We immediately made plans to fly to Oregon. Before we left we phoned the Terrills, who were in their motor home at Camp WiNeMa on the coast. They left camp at once and met us in Canby. Then for a week Jeff drove us in the motor home from Portland to Canby to Port Orford to Brookings and points in between. Lane died on Thursday before Memorial Day. Because of the holiday and because his suicide required police involvement, we couldn't get clearance for the funeral until the following Wednesday. So day after day we were together. All of us: Roy and Joy, Jeff and Joan, Grandma and Grandpa Whitney, Kim and her first husband Royce, Candy, Brian. An outsider wouldn't have been able to tell we weren't all blood family.

The truth is this: In spite of the awful circumstances, we drew deeply on the love that was holding us together. We cried and hugged and laughed and in every possible way helped one another limp through the ordeal. When it was over, we knew we had to get together again. Like next year. Thus our annual all-family vacation week was born. Lane's death had cemented us as one family in 1994 as Shawn's had in 1989. Our love for each other would reunite us in 1995 and has continued doing so every year since.

Let me jump out of sequence here. There was another unforeseen consequence of Jeff Terrill's fateful appearance in the tiny congregation of Villa Ridge Christian Church so long ago. Fast forward several decades. In 1997 Pacific Christian College had evolved into Hope International University. A couple of years later, thanks to a multimillion-dollar gift from Stan Fulton of Las Vegas, we were making plans to build the Lawson-Fulton Student Center[2], the only new building we constructed during my thirteen-year

2. The name needs explaining. Students thought the building was named for the president and vice president of HIU, LeRoy Lawson and Leroy Fulton. They probably had some choice comments to make about the egoism of the top administrators. But they were wrong.

When Stan Fulton (no relation to Leroy) made his generous gift, the HIU board agreed to name the building for him. I flew to Las Vegas to ask him to accept the board's

presidency. We had bought several others, but this would be a state-of-the-art gymnasium and multipurpose building. (The irony was not lost on some of my friends, who pointed out that the physical legacy of this totally nonathletic president would be a *gymnasium*.)

At about the same time we began searching for a new head of campus maintenance. I couldn't think of anyone who would do a better job than Jeff. He'd closed his business and bought another motor home. He and Joan had plans to travel around America for a year or two. From my point of view, that meant he was available! If he would, he could help the university immensely.

He would. So for three years we got to work together, during which time he scrubbed and polished our tattered campus and built the new student center. Jeff's a master in applying that old saw, "It's easier to ask forgiveness than to get permission." He and his immediate boss Laure Close had more than one disagreement. She wasn't alone. He overrode some of my cherished desires. He got forgiveness from both of us because he got the job done, and got it done with quality.

We were still there for each other.

14. Laughter Keeps You Together

I probably don't need to name this characteristic separately because you've already noted how often it's been mentioned on these pages. Everybody knows the old saw that "the family that prays together stays together." This is the corollary: The family that laughs together stays together. And another from *Reader's Digest*: "Laughter is the best medicine."

It is. Okay, here goes the preacher again. For years occasional visitors to the churches we've served have been impressed—and sometimes offended—by the congregational laughter. It strikes some as terribly irreverent. Church services should be solemn affairs, they insisted. I respectfully disagree with them. Church services should be serious affairs, I explain if

---

decision. He refused. In spite of my importuning, he remained adamant. He didn't want his name on the building. So I tried a different tack. Stan and I had often reminisced about his father, whom he admired. "Let us name the building in honor of your father," I proposed. He asked for time to think about it.

Within two days I received a note from Stan. "We'll name the building after our fathers." And it was so. I was embarrassed, because even this decision seemed self-serving on my part, but as I said, Stan was adamant. And it was his money.

they'll gave me a chance, but not solemn. Like singing and praying and communion and offering times, laughter belongs in church.

My rationale? It's a sign of belonging, of comfortable togetherness. You don't freely laugh in the presence of someone with whom you feel insecure, who hasn't accepted you, who holds you in judgment. Ours were nonjudgmental churches; we could laugh. Thus the Velcro family. We laugh a lot because we belong to each other. As I said above, teasing is our love language—and good-natured, love-based teasing always elicits laughter.

Afterword

Roy and Joy still enjoying life

"THEY ARE YOUR *VELCRO* family." That was Iris Armstrong's word for us. We adopted her term because it fits—and because we like it. We do stick together, like the real Velcro.

But what about *family*? What makes family *family*? I've been pondering this question for most of my life. During my youth I was an interested party in the gradual disintegration of my birth family. Like children everywhere, I simply took our togetherness for granted. I wasn't the only one. In our small town, Verne and Margery Lawson appeared to be happy enough, at least for the first few years. Much later, when Dad was reviewing with me what went wrong—yet again—he revealed that only six weeks into the

146

marriage Mom told him she didn't love him. So apparently it had always been shaky, but they shielded us children—until they couldn't shield us any longer. By my high school years it couldn't be hidden. Dad moved out of the bedroom more and more often. His hours at work grew longer and longer. Mom's spells of being "under the weather," as Dad explained it whenever she didn't want to go someplace with him, seemed increasingly suspicious. Then, after nineteen years of wedded nonbliss, it was over.

It was *over*. But isn't family supposed to be forever? What about that "'til death do us part" part? And what'll become of the children? Whose side should they take?

You know all those questions. My parents knew the questions. They just couldn't find the answer. So—I grew up in a blood family without Velcro.

How then was I, a *minister*, to define family? For three generations now I am the only member of my blood family who hasn't been divorced. (I usually add here, "It's Joy's fault. It's not as if I didn't give her just cause.") As a pastor I couldn't point to my own family and tell my parishioners, "This is how you do it." Because we were how you shouldn't do it. For that matter, I couldn't find many Biblical examples of how you do it, either.

At some point, when I was wrestling with the question of what makes family *family* the answer came to me. And it came from our Velcro family. What holds us together? What has made us so important to one another? My mind returned to the wedding vow, the vows my parents didn't keep. To Joy's and my wedding vows, which at times seemed to be the only thing that kept us together.

That's it! The vows. The promises. The word spoken to each other that was not to be broken. Here's the key to our Velcro family: "*We make promises to each other and we keep them.*" We love each other not because of, but in spite of. We're just not always all that loveable, none of us. Yet we are loved and we love. In spite of.

On these pages you've been reading the stories of people who know how to love with a love that doesn't let go, who have made promises—and kept them.

What's the future for this family? For several years I'd been asking myself this question. I wasn't the only one. More than one of the younger set have prophesied its demise. "When you and Joy are gone . . ." Once you hit eighty there's no denying you're now *old*. Our days are numbered, and these pretty blunt people don't mind reminding us.

However, there's now widespread agreement—even among the younger set—that Joy and I aren't indispensable. As you've picked up on these pages, the ties that bind are strong, and others are stepping into the leadership roles even as Grandma and Grandpa are increasingly to be found in the audience, cheering. As in any healthy biological family, a Velcro family is stronger than any one individual. Grandma and I will attend every gathering we can get to until we can't get to any more—but there have already been reunions without us. And we're glad. Nothing is more gratifying than knowing the people you love, love the other people you love.

We used to sing an old hymn that I don't hear anymore, which is a pity. It goes like this:

> O Love that will not let me go,
> I rest my weary soul in thee;
> I give thee back the life I owe,
> That in thine ocean depths its flow
> May richer, fuller be.

It's about the love of God, of course, but it comes to my mind often when I'm thinking about this family. Here a bunch of admittedly far-less-than-perfect individuals, struggling to make themselves whole out of broken pieces, have experienced unconditional love. We've learned how much more rewarding it is to say *us* instead of *me, ours* in place of *mine*, to put up with the stresses in our togetherness instead of escaping to some imaginary tension-free apartness. In one another we actually do find a kind of rest from weariness, a depth that can't be found in pure individuality. We are richer, fuller because we have one another.

That love that doesn't let go won't let go when Grandpa and Grandma are no longer here. We'll have moved from the playing field to the bleachers to the Biblical "cloud of witnesses." We will still be cheering the players, but from a heavenly distance.